A Companion to

The Grapes of Wrath

Assembled and Edited by

Warren French

PENGUIN BOOKS

PENGUIN BOOKS
Published by the Penguin Group
Viking Penguin Inc., 40 West 23rd Street,
New York, New York 10010, U.S.A.
Penguin Books Ltd, 27 Wrights Lane,
London W8 5TZ, England
Penguin Books Australia Ltd, Ringwood,
Victoria, Australia
Penguin Books Canada Ltd, 2801 John Street,
Markham, Ontario, Canada L3R 1B4
Penguin Books (N.Z.) Ltd, 182–190 Wairau Road,
Auckland 10, New Zealand

Penguin Books Ltd, Registered Offices:
Harmondsworth, Middlesex, England

First published in the United States of America by
Viking Penguin Inc. 1963
Published in Penguin Books 1989

10 9 8 7 6 5 4 3 2 1

LIBRARY OF CONGRESS CATALOGING IN PUBLICATION DATA
A Companion to The grapes of wrath / edited by Warren French.
    p. cm.
Reprint. Originally published: New York: Viking Press, 1963.
Bibliography: p.
Includes index.
    1. Steinbeck, John, 1902–1968. Grapes of wrath. I. French,
Warren G., 1922–   . II. Steinbeck, John, 1902–1968. Grapes of wrath.
PS3537.T3234G85 1989
813'.52—dc19   88-32759
ISBN 0 14 01.1987 6

Printed in the United States of America
Set in Janson and Times Roman

To the memory of

Edgar F. Bennett

*who taught me and many others
to appreciate* The Grapes of Wrath

Contents

Foreword

NEARLY A QUARTER OF A CENTURY AFTER THE APPEARANCE of *The Grapes of Wrath,* John Steinbeck was awarded the Nobel Prize for literature. Although some scoffers had dismissed *The Grapes of Wrath* as mere timely propaganda when it headed the best-seller lists in 1939, the novel more than twenty years later has overshadowed its author's own later work, as well as much of the less dynamic fiction of the confused postwar era.

Most controversial "social novels" date quickly; in a decade or two they become simply historical documents, to be forgotten long before the events that inspired them. Steinbeck's novel, however, is today better known to many young readers than the tragic situations it portrays. It is a shock to realize that a whole generation has grown up without knowledge of the dust bowl, the migrant problem, and the rise during the 1930s of Fascism abroad and at home. Instead of turning to *The Grapes of Wrath* merely as the portrait of a period, these young readers have their interest aroused in the troublesome years before their birth by one of its living artistic landmarks.

Steinbeck's novel inspires its present-day readers to ask questions that the novel—quite properly—does not answer: What was the dust bowl? Who were the "Okies"? What became of them? How was Steinbeck's angry novel received? Is it "just propaganda" or enduring art? This *Companion* is designed to answer these questions—to provide the background for the novelist's art.

As answers, I have given wherever possible authoritative and readable documents by first-hand observers. Where no such documents exist, I present the answers I myself have pieced together during the dozen years that I have studied and taught *The Grapes of Wrath*. The first section of the book deals with the geographical, historical, and sociological background of the novel; the second with its reception in 1939; the third with its enduring reputation. This *Companion* will, I hope, prove useful both to those who seek to learn of these matters for the first time and to those who wish to refresh their memories. It may be read straight through as a panoramic account of some great social issues of the thirties and the novel that grew out of them; or it can be dipped into as a reference book by those seeking answers to specific questions about the novel or the period.

The idea for this *Companion* came to me as I mulled over questions posed by undergraduates at the Universities of Kentucky and Florida; it is my response to their healthy curiosity. I am greatly indebted to Pascal Covici, John Steinbeck's long-time friend and editor, for recognizing the need for this book and encouraging me to go ahead with it. I am grateful also to all those who have granted me permission to reprint their work, and especially to M. M. Leighton, retired chief of the Illinois State Geological Survey, who encouraged me to edit his essay on soil drift; and to Carey McWilliams, editor of *The Nation* and perhaps our greatest authority on the migrant problem, who kindly reviewed my discussion of what became of the "Okies" and made several invaluable suggestions from his own intimate knowledge of the California situation. I also acknowledge with deepest gratitude the help of Bob Griffin and Bill Freedman; I could never have assembled the material here presented if they had not often interrupted their own studies at Berkeley and Chicago to pursue the fading records of the 1930s for me.

I also wish to thank the Kansas State University Bureau of General Research for providing the time and assistance necessary to complete this project. The Bureau's grant has enabled me to employ the able services of Wilfred Dvorak in assembling, checking, and proofreading this material.

WARREN FRENCH

Manhattan, Kansas
January 1963

PART I

Background

CHAPTER 1

What Was the Dust Bowl?

H. L. Mencken in a footnote to the first supplement (1945) to his monumental *The American Language* traces the term "dust bowl" to an Associated Press dispatch sent by staff writer Robert Geiger from Guymon, Oklahoma, on April 15, 1935. Geiger later refused to accept a reward offered by Albert Law, editor of the Dalhart (Texas) *Texan,* for information about the first appearance of the term in print, since the reporter thought he might have picked it up from someone. It could not have been in use long when he wrote his dispatch, however, for it described a relatively recent phenomenon, the seriousness of which Americans were just beginning to recognize in the spring of 1935.

Midwestern dust had begun blowing a year and a half earlier. On November 12 and 13, 1933, an enormous cloud of dust had covered an area from Texas to South Dakota, forming a triangle with its apex at Milwaukee. However, few observers saw in this event a portent of the future. The *New York Times Index* for 1933 contains no reference to dust storms, and the *Literary Digest,* a genteel weekly news-magazine that foundered during the Depression, described the storm as simply "a freakish phenomenon that darkened the sky and frightened people."

The dust, however, did not stop blowing. Day after day,

in Texas and Oklahoma—especially their panhandles—and most of Kansas, eastern Colorado, Wyoming, and New Mexico, the sun was hidden by choking masses of fine dust. Thinner clouds covered Missouri, Iowa, and Arkansas and reached as far east as Michigan and as far south as Tennessee and Louisiana. On March 15, 1935, the air over Kansas was filled with swirling dust so thick that when seven-year-old Khile Salmon wandered from his home near Hays, he was suffocated before he could be found. The Texas Senate wore gas masks during its sessions on April 10 and 11. The *New York Times* reported on April 20, 1935, that the dust had been blowing constantly for more than a month and doing millions of dollars' worth of damage to newly planted crops.

Accounts by two scientists help us to reconstruct this terrifying period. Ivan Ray Tannehill, an assistant chief of the Forecast Division of the United States Weather Bureau during the years of the first dust storms, gives a vivid picture of dust-bowl conditions that places the storms in historical perspective. M. M. Leighton, at that time Chief of the Illinois State Geological Survey, explains the geological reasons for the storms.

The most important fact about the dust storms, however, was not scientific but human: their tragic effect upon people seeking livelihood on the stricken Midwestern farms. As *The Grapes of Wrath* shows, many disheartened farmers were driven from their land or left voluntarily. But some tenacious families—often descendants of the pioneers who had conquered the plains—refused to be uprooted. A glimpse into the lives of some of these individuals during this trying period is afforded by a number of letters written by Mrs. Caroline A. Henderson, of Eva, Oklahoma, to a

friend in Maryland. These letters offer first-hand evidence
of the incredible conditions against which the human spirit
can contend, and of the foolish pride that makes disaster
worse by seeking to conceal the truth about it.

Ivan Ray Tannehill
Dusters and Black Blizzards

The United States is well fed. That is because a considerable
part of our country nearly always gets plenty of rain and other
forms of precipitation. Under normal conditions we produce
more food than we need; nevertheless, drought has serious
consequences. Any important widespread deficiency of rainfall
in the United States, even for only a year or two, strikes at
the very foundation of our national security as does nothing
else except war or revolution. This fact has been impressed on
us twice within the last sixty years when, in the depths of
national depression, we were severely shocked by what we
thought at the time was a broad-scale change to a drier climate.

Some early maps had the words "Great American Desert"
written across the Western Range, including the plains in the
western parts of Nebraska, Kansas, and Texas. These words
disappeared from our maps when we discovered that these vast
areas are suitable for grazing and when the distribution of rainfall became more favorable after the middle of the last century.
Following the Civil War, for a period of twenty years, there
was increasing rainfall in the Great Plains. The generally accepted idea was that cultivation of the land had increased the
rainfall. It was thought that the power of the soil to absorb

From *Drought: Its Causes and Effects*, by Ivan Ray Tannehill
(Princeton, N.J.: Princeton University Press, 1948), copyright 1948
by Princeton University Press. Portions of Chapter 1 (pp. 10-12)
and Chapter 4 (pp. 44-51) are reprinted here by permission of the
Princeton University Press.

moisture had improved and that the increase in soil moisture in turn caused an increase in the rainfall. Later this idea proved to be mistaken. Droughts became more severe, and now it is thought that cultivation had little to do with the amount of rainfall.

Our first experience with serious widespread drought started after the middle of the 1880s, when the rainfall for the nation as a whole began to diminish. For three consecutive years in the nineties it was far below normal. It culminated in the great drought of 1894 and 1895. We had never known anything like it. It may have happened before we settled the vast interior of the continent, but this was the first great drought to put fear in our hearts. . . .

Occupation of the Great Plains for agriculture began about 1885. The settlers made a livelihood by crop farming during three or four years of fairly good rainfall. Then there were three lean years and the great drought of 1894 brought complete crop failure and disaster. As many as ninety per cent of the settlers abandoned their farms in some areas.

In the big drought of the nineties there was a great deal of dust. The following are notes selected from the official records of the Weather Bureau in the early nineties at Dodge City in southwestern Kansas:

April 8, 1890: At 10 a. m. the dust in the air was so dense that objects could not be distinguished 100 yards off. No one who could possibly remain indoors was on the street.

August 13, 1892: The wind raised such a cloud of dust that it was impossible to see over 150 feet ahead.

April 6, 1893: The dust was blinding and was deposited so thickly on office furniture that everything looked as though it were covered by a layer of dirt prepared for a hot-bed.

In the years following the drought of the nineties, there was more rainfall. Grama-buffalo sod replaced the bare fields, and the plains healed. Then came World War I and high prices. Crop farming was resumed on a large scale, and tractors and other labor-saving machines were introduced. Grain farming had spread widely by the end of the wet years from 1905 to 1915.

Drier years came. It grew steadily warmer with few reversals. These were the warmest years in the history of the Great Plains. Drought seemed to be chronic. Wells were dug deeper and deeper until there were cases where it took a gallon of gasoline for power to pump a gallon of water. The subsoil moisture was depleted to a great depth.

The desert seemed to be spreading into the Plains. By 1935 topsoil was blowing in tremendous quantities. At intervals there were winds of high velocity with spiraling masses of powdery dust. As time went on the dust, which was coarse in the beginning, was blown again and again and became exceedingly fine.

Dust drifted into feed stacks and covered the pastures. In some places, livestock died from starvation and suffocation. Wet blankets were placed over doors and windows. People covered their faces with wet cloths. Static electricity rendered automobile ignition systems useless. Motorists were stranded until the blows ceased temporarily, and then the ignition systems worked again. Many dragged chains to dissipate the electricity. Ranch homes were deserted. Drifts piled up and stopped trains and automobiles. Planes were grounded. Driving sand removed paint from automobiles and pitted windshields. During some of the storms, artificial light was needed at noon. Business was suspended. In some cases it was so dark from dust that pedestrians collided in the streets.

These conditions occurred at intervals for several years. At the end of March 1936 there was snow and in some places flurries of rain with the dust. There were mud showers, and muddy snow in the form of balls fell in north-central Colorado.

Drought brings other troubles. The grasshopper is one of the worst. Dry, warm weather is favorable for hatching grasshoppers, and a continued spell may bring a serious outbreak. . . . For the five-year drought period from 1934 to 1938 the losses from destruction of crops by grasshoppers was estimated at approximately $315,753,000.

Dust storms still continued in 1939, but the "dust bowl" had shrunk to about one-fifth of its original size, from fifty million acres at its worst to about ten million acres. There was a national deficiency of rainfall in 1939 which temporarily revived the dust storms, but more rain came in succeeding years and the Plains had returned nearly to normal in time to meet the demands of the nation in World War II.

M. M. Leighton

Geology of Soil Drifting on the Great Plains

No subject is more important to mankind than that of husbanding natural resources. Among natural resources, none is more important than soils. Directly or indirectly they provide us with food; their well-being determines our pleasure and comfort; their fixity—or lack of it—has profound effects on our health. Without soil in virtually stable condition civilization cannot exist.

All this is everyday knowledge; to some degree it has been apparent for many centuries. But to know is one thing; to act is another. As [P.B.] Sears has shown in *Deserts on the March,* human settlement and land use have led, without significant

From *The Scientific Monthly,* XLVI (July 1938), 22-33. Originally a paper presented in a symposium on "Scientific Aspects of the Control of Drifting Soils" before the American Association for the Advancement of Science, Dr. Leighton's article has been condensed especially for this volume, and is reprinted here by permission of the author and of the American Association for the Advancement of Science.

exception, to wholesale wastage of soils. This waste has gone so far that the need for conservation is immediate and pressing; it challenges any enlightened people. Even in the most fertile areas of new countries such as ours, the natural productive capacity of the soil has been greatly reduced by prevailing methods of grazing and farming. This reduction has dollars-and-cents importance. It also presents a grave problem which affects our national future.

The drifting of soils by wind is one very serious phase of the matter. In the Great Plains, our once-wild West, drifting already is a menace to soil resources of the great wheatlands. It is almost as threatening in the grazing regions. Travelers who cross the panhandle of Texas, the sage plains of Wyoming, or the grasslands of Montana will see broad stretches whose value is sinking to almost nothing as winds carry soil away.

Spectacular and overwhelming as it is in the Great Plains, soil drifting is important in even the Central Lowlands. During dry seasons, strong winds pile ridges of black, fertile soil along fences and hedgerows of Illinois and Iowa. Flat stretches of plowed land and the plowed brows of slopes suffer alike from air currents, which first carry and then deposit the material in those ridges. Effects may seem trifling during a decade, appearing negligible to the average layman. But their cumulative results will become disastrous unless intelligent practices reduce drifting until it corresponds to the natural rate of soil renewal.

Soil-drifting is a widespread process, affecting many different types of land. In North America, however, it has specially characterized the region which we term the Great Plains, long recognized as a wide belt of high country which slopes eastward from the Rockies to the Central Lowlands. Popularly, the name Great Plains is associated with monotonous landscapes, short grasses, and rainfall of less than 20 inches. In general this conception is valid today. The Plains contrast sharply with the prairies or "long-grass country" which bound them on the east. That boundary runs through western Minnesota and Iowa, eastern Nebraska, east-central Kansas, and central Oklahoma and Texas. Throughout much of its length it is marked by low eastward-facing escarpments which are continuous in some places, ragged in others, and in some have been transformed into low belts of hills. In Nebraska and South Dakota, however, this boundary is indefinite. From elevations of 1200 to 1500 feet along this eastern border, the land rises to heights of 4000 to 5000 feet in its western belt, called the High Plains. Streams which originate in the mountains flow eastward and southeastward across the sloping country to the Mississippi and the Gulf of Mexico. Through long ages, these streams and their tributaries have cut valleys, transforming the surface into a landscape which is much more irregular than it generally seems. Only the Llano Estacado, in the Texas panhandle, and uplands near the Kansas-Colorado boundary remain as extensive, level areas almost untouched by erosion. The former comprise 20,000 square miles whose surface has been called by [N.M.] Fenneman, in *Physiography of Western North America*, "as flat as any land surface in nature."

Except in regions where crystalline rocks reach the surface, both the Great Plains and the Central Lowlands are underlain by sediments. In the Lowlands these stratified rocks may be thin: there are places in South Dakota and Minnesota where they amount to less than a hundred feet. Throughout most of the Plains, however, sediments are thousands of feet thick, include many kinds of rock, and are grouped into formations of many different ages. These formations outcrop in a narrow belt near the mountains and over great areas in Texas, Oklahoma, and Kansas, as well as other Plains states, and these outcrops have provided material for extensive areas of soil. The pre-Tertiary strata (those which are more than sixty million years old) have been bowed downward into a basin-like structure whose rocks dip steeply eastward near the mountains but have gentle westward dips on the east side of the basin. Their variations in hardness, as well as their structure, are expressed in the remarkable linear, subparallel escarpments and ridges of eastern Kansas and in steep, high "hogbacks" near the Rocky Mountain front near Boulder, Denver, and Colorado Springs. Most of these tilted rocks are resistant, but some of the Cretaceous shales which outcrop in Colorado and Wyoming, as well as Triassic "red beds" of the Texas-Oklahoma panhandles, yield readily to erosion by the strong, turbulent winds that are common in those areas.

The older and more indurated strata are popularly called bedrock. In large areas of western Texas, the panhandle of Oklahoma and western and central Kansas, and in most of Nebraska, the bedrock is covered with relatively young, unconsolidated sediments. These are the Tertiary deposits, which were washed from the rejuvenated Rocky Mountains and deposited on the Great Plains. Erosion has carved them into hills and valleys and reduced them to remnants along their fringing borders. Throughout considerable areas the surface soils have been made from them. In some places both the soils and some of the parent deposits are readily subject to wind erosion, especially where they are sandy or silty.

Other very extensive areas are covered with loose, incoherent deposits of windblown silt whose origin dates back thousands rather than millions of years. These are the loess deposits of northern and western Kansas and eastern and southern Nebraska; they also extend over large parts of Iowa, Missouri, Illinois, and adjacent territory. This loess consists of old wind-transported and wind-laid dust deposits which were formed at various times, chiefly during the Glacial Period.

In the northwestern part of Nebraska, an area of dune sand, amounting to about 24,000 square miles, is known as the "Sand Hills." There are other, though smaller, sand areas in Colorado, Kansas, Oklahoma, and Texas. Some or all of them may also have contributed material for loess deposits bordering these tracts.

The chief sources of recent dust storms are areas within the High Plains and in regions just east of them. The High Plains lie on the dry, lee side of the Rocky Mountains, from which they are separated by the rough Colorado Piedmont. The climate of both regions belongs to the dry continental type, in contrast to the moist continental climate of the Mississippi Valley states. According to records of the United States Weather Bureau, summarized in the Atlas of American Agriculture, the average annual precipitation throughout most of the High Plains ranges from 15 to 20 inches. In the larger part of the upper Mississippi Valley it is 30 to 40 inches, while 50 to 60 inches of rain fall on the lower Mississippi states. Even in March, April, and May, which are moist months, precipitation on the High Plains is almost half what it is in the upper Mississippi Valley. Crop production west of the 100th meridian therefore requires either irrigation or dry-farming methods.

Low precipitation here is accompanied by notably high evaporation. On the average, the winds of the High Plains also blow faster than those east of the 100th meridian. These strong, dry winds intensify the aridity caused by light precipitation. They therefore limit vegetative cover, producing biologic as well as climatic conditions which favor the drifting of soil. When winds become very strong—A. H. Joel in the United States Department of Agriculture *Technical Bulletin* 556 (1937) records velocities of 40 to 65 at Amarillo, Texas—only soil which has very effective cover can resist the impetus to move.

The recent dust storms were the natural results of deficient rainfall, depleted subsoil moisture, and greatly reduced vegetation in a region of loose, dry soil and strong, turbulent winds. These factors prevailed in both the northern and southern portions of the High Plains. According to the Weather Bureau, there was an increasing deficiency of moisture at St. Paul during the twenty-two years preceding 1934. From 1926 to 1933, the average annual rainfall was three inches less than the normal amount.

No such prolonged period of moisture deficiency seems to have affected the southern High Plains, although in 1933 the annual precipitation at Dalhart, Texas, was 10.14 inches and in

1934 it sank to only 9.78 inches—slightly more than half the average over a period of twenty-seven years. In the first ten months of 1936, rainfall in North Dakota was 50 per cent of normal; in South Dakota, 52 per cent; in Montana, 75 per cent; in Nebraska, 68 per cent; in Kansas, 69 per cent; and in Oklahoma, 70 per cent. These deficiencies reduced crop yields and also brought grave harm to the protective vegetation on soils.

In addition to their serious damage to the soils, dust storms have brought tragedy and loss to human beings. They have destroyed lives; created discomfort and illness among thousands; killed livestock; made highways impassable; ruined motors; damaged the contents of stores, factories, and homes; buried orchards, fields, and gardens; and disrupted commercial production. They also have brought darkness in midday, and have spread mud-rains far and wide over the country.

During March and April 1935 there were 47 days on which visibility at Amarillo, Texas, was limited to six miles or less; during the majority of storms it was one mile or less and during six storms it was less than five hundred feet. Fifteen storms lasted longer than twenty-four hours, and four lasted fifty-five hours or more. After the dust reached the higher levels of the atmosphere it was carried hundreds of miles. In eastern Illinois there were days when the atmosphere held so much dust that the sky was murky and the sun shone red. Some of this dust was carried even to the Atlantic Coast.

If such dust storms were to become the rule, they might have even other serious consequences. The interception of heat rays from the sun would retard normal heating of the earth's surface, reduce average temperatures, diminish plant growth, and adversely affect weather conditions other than those of temperature.

Contrary to the common impression, dust storms of the 1930s are not the only destructive ones that have swept the Great Plains. The subnormal moisture conditions which set the stage for these storms occur in cycles. Climate has its pulsations on both small and large scales and over various periods of time.

Any plan devised to offset wind erosion or soil drifting must consider cyclic changes. It must also take into account the fact that soil tillage over a period of years reduces the humus content, unless special treatment is given, while lowered humus content, in turn, reduces the moisture-retaining capacities of soils. In consequence of these changes, recent dust storms were more destructive and widespread than they otherwise would have been. The dust storms of future dry cycles will grow even more destructive if reduction of the soil's humus continues.

The geologist looks upon the problem of wind erosion in the Great Plains from a viewpoint which differs from that of the non-geologist. Every earth historian knows that dust storms of the Glacial Period were greater and more protracted than those of the 1930s. He also knows that certain definite conditions brought those storms to a close, introducing a long period of soil stability. As for dust from the Sand Hills, it apparently was sorted out and removed during the interval of transition from the moist glacial to the dry postglacial climate. This change apparently was so rapid that there was only a brief period between the death of protective plants that had grown during moist times and the arrival of drought-resistant species. During that break the Sand Hills were unprotected from the high winds that swept across them and continued eastward beyond the Missouri. When drought-resistant plants became established, wind erosion again became trifling. Since that happened, soils have formed extensively, proving that relatively stable conditions prevailed until the white man arrived.

The dust storms which we have just considered ended long before men brought farming and grazing into the Great Plains. Nevertheless, they allow us to draw four conclusions of value to those who now are attempting to mend the damage wrought by unwise use of the land:

1. Dust storms will occur in even a moist climate if broad areas of fine rock material, without vegetative cover, are exposed to the wind. This is true whether the exposure is due to

natural causes or to the turning of the sod by man's plow. In the Middle West today, winds are removing soil from plowed fields, though more slowly than they take it from the dry Great Plains and the semiarid High Plains.

2. The general prevalence of a definite soil profile over the Great Plains, and even the High Plains, shows that their climate is not too dry for a general vegetative cover to develop if it is permitted to do so. Man's activities, carried on without a knowledge of or regard for the economy of nature, are responsible for dust storms of modern times.

3. In the High Plains, and under some conditions of soil and topography on the relatively low plains, the opposing factors are so nearly critically balanced that man must act with intelligence and skill if he is not to lose his greatest resource. If he follows proper methods, there is hope for the "dust bowl" of the High Plains as well as for the fertile Central Lowlands.

4. The short climatic cycles probably produced local but not widespread wind erosion under virgin conditions. But man's work is a new and powerful geologic factor which must be used with caution, especially during the drier parts of these minor climatic cycles, lest it result in soil-drifting and deposition on a nationally destructive scale.

Caroline A. Henderson
Letters from the Dust Bowl

Eva, Oklahoma
June 30, 1935

My dear Evelyn:

Your continued interest in our effort to "tie a knot in the end of the rope and hang on" is most stimulating. Our recent transition from rain-soaked eastern Kansas with its green pas-

From *The Atlantic Monthly*, CLVII (May 1936), 540-551. Selections from Mrs. Henderson's "Letters from the Dust Bowl" are reprinted here by permission of *The Atlantic Monthly*.

tures, luxuriant foliage, abundance of flowers, and promise of a generous harvest, to the dust-covered desolation of No Man's Land was a difficult change to crowd into one short day's travel. Eleanor had laid aside the medical books for a time. Wearing our shade hats, with handkerchiefs tied over our faces and Vaseline in our nostrils, we have been trying to rescue our home from the accumulations of wind-blown dust which penetrates wherever air can go. It is an almost hopeless task, for there is rarely a day when at some time the dust clouds do not roll over. "Visibility" approaches zero and everything is covered again with a siltlike deposit which may vary in depth from a film to actual ripples on the kitchen floor. I keep oiled cloths on the window sills and between the upper and lower sashes. They help just a little to retard or collect the dust. Some seal the windows with the gummed-paper strips used in wrapping parcels, but no method is fully effective. We buy what appears to be red cedar sawdust with oil added to use in sweeping our floors, and do our best to avoid inhaling the irritating dust.

In telling you of these conditions I realize that I expose myself to charges of disloyalty to this western region. A good Kansas friend suggests that we should imitate the Californian attitude toward earthquakes and keep to ourselves what we know about dust storms. Since the very limited rains of May in this section gave some slight ground for renewed hope, optimism has been the approved policy. Printed articles or statements by journalists, railroad officials, and secretaries of small-town Chambers of Commerce have heralded too enthusiastically the return of prosperity to the drought region. And in our part of the country that is the one durable basis for any prosperity whatever. There is nothing else to build upon. But you wished to know the truth, so I am telling you the actual situation, though I freely admit that the facts are themselves often contradictory and confusing.

Early in May, with no more grass or even weeds on our 640

acres than on your kitchen floor, and even the scanty remnants of dried grasses from last year cut off and blown away, we decided, like most of our neighbors, to ship our cattle to grass in the central part of the state. We sent 27 head, retaining here the heifers coming fresh this spring. The shipping charge on our part of the carload was $46. Pasture costs us $7.00 for a cow and calf for the season and $5.00 for a yearling. Whether this venture brings profit or loss depends on whether the cattle make satisfactory gains during the summer and whether prices remain reasonable or fall back to the level that most people would desire. We farmers here in the United States might as well recognize that we are a minority group, and that the prevailing interest of the nation as a whole is no longer agricultural. Hay for the horses and the heifers remaining here cost us $23 per ton, brought by truck from eastern Oklahoma.

The day after we shipped the cattle, the long drought was temporarily broken by the first effective moisture in many months—about one and one-quarter inches in two or three gentle rains. All hope of a wheat crop had been abandoned by March or April.

Contrary to many published reports, a good many people had left this country either temporarily or permanently before any rains came. And they were not merely "drifters," as is frequently alleged. In May a friend in the southwestern county of Kansas voluntarily sent me a list of the people who had already left their immediate neighborhood or were packed up and ready to go. The list included 109 persons in 26 families, substantial people, most of whom had been in that locality over ten years, and some as long as forty years. In these families there had been two deaths from dust pneumonia. Others in the neighborhood were ill at that time. Fewer actual residents have left our neighborhood, but on a sixty-mile trip yesterday to procure tractor repairs we saw many pitiful reminders of broken hopes and apparently wasted effort. Little abandoned homes where people had drilled deep wells for the precious water, had set trees and vines, built reservoirs, and fenced in gardens—with everything now walled in or half buried by banks of drifted soil —told a painful story of loss and disappointment. I grieved especially over one lonely plum thicket buried to the tips of the twigs, and a garden with a fence closely built of boards for wind protection, now enclosing only a hillock of dust covered with the blue-flowered bull nettles which no winds or sands discourage.

It might give you some notion of our great "open spaces" if I tell you that on the sixty-mile trip, going by a state road over which our mail comes from the railroad, and coming back by a federal highway, we encountered only one car, and no other vehicles of any sort. And this was on Saturday, the farmers' marketing day!

The coming of the long-desired rain gave impetus to the federal projects for erosion control. Plans were quickly made, submitted to groups of farmers in district gatherings, and put into operation without delay.

The proposition was that, in order to encourage the immediate listing of abandoned wheat ground and other acreage so as to cut down wind erosion, the federal government would contribute ten cents per acre toward the expense of fuel and oil for tractors or feed for horses, if the farmers would agree to list not less than one-fourth of the acreage on contour lines. Surveys were made promptly for all farmers signing contracts for either contour listing or terracing. The latest report states that within the few weeks since the program was begun in our county 299,986 acres have been plowed or listed on these contour lines —that is, according to the lay of the land instead of on straight lines with right-angled turns as has been the usual custom.

The plan has been proposed and carried through here as a matter of public policy for the welfare of all without reproach or humiliation to anyone. It should be remembered that 1935 is the fourth successive year of drought and crop failure through a great part of the High Plains region, and the hopelessly low prices for the crop of 1931 gave no chance to build up reserves for future needs. If the severe critics of all who in any way join in government plans for the saving of homes and the restoration of farms to a productive basis could only understand how vital a human problem is here considered, possibly their censures might be less bitter and scornful.

At any rate the contour listing has been done over extensive areas. If rains come to carry forward the feed crops now just struggling up in the furrows, the value of the work can be appraised. The primary intention of the plan for contour listing is to distribute rainfall evenly over the fields and prevent its running off to one end of the field or down the road to some creek or drainage basin. It is hoped that the plan will indirectly tend to lessen wind erosion by promoting the growth of feed crops, restoration of humus to denuded surfaces, and some protection through standing stubbles and the natural coverage of weeds and unavoidable wastes. One great contributing cause of the terrible dust storms of the last two years has been the pitiful bareness of the fields resulting from the long drought.

I am not wise enough to forecast the result. We have had two most welcome rains in June—three-quarters of an inch and one-half inch. Normally these should have been of the utmost benefit, though they by no means guarantee an abundant feed crop from our now sprouting seeds as many editorial writers have decreed, and they do nothing toward restoring subsoil moisture. Actually the helpful effects of the rains have been for us and for other people largely destroyed by the drifting soil from abandoned, unworked lands around us. It fills the air and our eyes and noses and throats, and, worst of all, our furrows, where tender shoots are coming to the surface only to be buried by the smothering silt from the fields of rugged individualists who persist in their right to do nothing.

A fairly promising piece of barley has been destroyed for us by the merciless drift from the same field whose sands have practically buried the little mulberry hedge which has long sheltered our buildings from the northwest winds. Large spaces in our pastures are entirely bare in spite of the rains. Most of the green color, where there is any grazing, is due to the pestilent Russian thistles rather than to grass. Our little locust grove which we cherished for so many years has become a small pile of fence posts. With trees and vines and flowers all around you, you can't imagine how I miss that little green shaded spot in the midst of the desert glare.

Naturally you will wonder why we stay where conditions are so extremely disheartening. Why not pick up and leave as so many others have done? It is a fair question, but a hard one to answer.

Recently I talked with a young university graduate of very superior attainments. He took the ground that in such a case sentiment could and should be disregarded. He may be right. Yet I cannot act or feel or think as if the experiences of our twenty-seven years of life together had never been. And they are all bound up with the little corner to which we have given our continued and united efforts. To leave voluntarily—to break all these closely knit ties for the sake of a possibly greater comfort elsewhere—seems like defaulting on our task. We may *have* to leave. We can't hold out indefinitely without some return from the land, some source of income, however small. But I think I can never go willingly or without pain that as yet seems unendurable.

There are also practical considerations that serve to hold us here, for the present. Our soil is excellent. We need only a little rain—less than in most places—to make it productive. No one who remembers the wheat crops of 1926, 1929, 1931, can possibly regard this as permanently submarginal land. The newer methods of farming suggest possibilities of better control of moisture in the future. Our entire equipment is adapted to the type of farming suitable for this country and would have to be replaced at great expense with the tools needed in some other locality. We have spent so much in trying to keep our land from blowing away that it looks foolish to walk off and leave it, when somewhat more favorable conditions seem now to "cast their shadows before." I scarcely need to tell you that there is no use in thinking of either renting or selling farm property here at present. It is just a place to stand on—if we can keep the taxes paid—and work and hope for a better day. We could realize nothing whatever from all our years of struggle with which to make a fresh start.

We long for the garden and little chickens, the trees and birds and wild flowers of the years gone by. Perhaps if we do our part these good things may return some day, for others if not for ourselves.

Will joins me in earnest hopes for your recovery. The dust has been particularly aggravating to his bronchial trouble, but he keeps working on. A great reddish-brown dust cloud is rising now from the southeast, so we must get out and do our night work before it arrives. Our thoughts go with you.

January 28, 1936

Dear Evelyn:

. . . As you know . . . wisely or otherwisely, this region has permitted wheat growing to become its main concern. The wheat situation around us is so varied and precarious as to be most difficult of appraisal. Our own acreage is fairly typical of the general condition. We have a little wheat that came up in September, made a fair start, and for a time furnished pasturage for the small calves. A part of it was early smothered out by the drift from nearby fields. Part of it would yet respond to abundant moisture if that were to come. Much of the early-sown wheat did not come up. Some of the seed sprouted and died before reaching the surface. Other portions remained dry until sprouted by a light rain in December. Most of that still lies dormant waiting for warmth to promote its growth. Large areas were drilled after the December rain, with varying results as to germination.

After the four-to-six-inch snow of early January, the editor of our county paper was asked by the United Press for a candid report of actual conditions. His estimate allowed the county as a whole a 25-per-cent chance; not, if I understood him, a fair chance for a 25-per-cent crop, but about one chance in four for anything at all. His statement showed that fall and winter precipitation so far had been a trifle over half the normal amount for that time of year. And you must try to remember that a failure this year would mean five in succession for a large part of the high plains region. So our great problem here is production, after all. You can readily see that the conditions I have so hastily outlined promise no protection against the ravages of dust storms if the spring winds rage as in previous years.

On the whole it is not surprising that here and there some bitterness should have been felt and expressed, perhaps immoderately, over the recent AAA decision in the Supreme Court.* People here, businessmen as well as the farmers themselves, realize that the benefit payments under the AAA and the wage payments from federal work projects are all that have saved a large territory here from abandonment. A December statement by the Soil Conservation service reports an area in five states, including part or all of sixty-eight counties and 87,900 square miles of territory, as in need of active measures for protection and control of the dust-storm menace. Mr. Bennett, director of the service, regards this as the greatest "physical problem facing the country today." I was astonished to find by a little primary arithmetic that the area involved is equal to that of all the New England states, with New Jersey and Maryland and about half of Delaware added for good measure.

The desolation of the countryside would admittedly have meant the ruin of the small towns, entirely dependent as they

* The court had ruled the Agricultural Adjustment Act unconstitutional.—ED.

are upon country patronage. It will also mean—if it must ever be abandoned through utter exhaustion of resources and sheer inability to hang on any longer—a creeping eastward into more settled and productive territory of the danger and losses originating in the arid wastelands. It is a problem now that no merely individual action can handle successfully. . . .

Farmers are not asking for special favors. They ask only an even chance as compared with other workers. But people don't understand.

Perhaps the many books on pioneer life with the usual successful and happy outcome have helped to give a wrong impression and perpetuate the idea that country people live on wild game and fish and fruits and in general on the free bounty of heaven. Many people have no idea of the cash expense of operating a farm today, or the work and planning required to keep the wheels going round, to say nothing of a decent living or suitable education for the children. This year we are keeping a separate account of expenses for car, truck, and tractor, all of which are old and frequently in need of repair. I fear we shall be horrified and discouraged by the close of the year. Not that I should willingly return to the long, slow trips of fifteen miles to town in a jolting wagon. Not that I want to take it out of the flesh and blood of horses in the hot heavy work of seed time and harvest—if they come again. But we can't combine the modern methods of work with the income of our early pioneering, when $200 used to cover all of a year's expense. . . .

March 8, 1936

Dear Evelyn;

Since I wrote to you, we have had several bad days of wind and dust. On the worst one recently, old sheets stretched over door and window openings, and sprayed with kerosene, quickly became black and helped a little to keep down the irritating dust in our living rooms. Nothing that you see or hear or read will be likely to exaggerate the physical discomfort or material losses due to these storms. Less emphasis is usually given to the mental effect, the confusion of mind resulting from the overthrow of all plans for improvement or normal farm work, and the difficulty of making other plans, even in a tentative way. To give just one specific example: the paint has been literally scoured from our buildings by the storms of this and previous years; we should by all means try to "save the surface"; but who knows when we might safely undertake such a project? The pleasantest morning may be a prelude to an afternoon when the "dust devils" all unite in one hideous onslaught. The combination of fresh paint with a real dust storm is not pleasing to contemplate.

The prospects for a wheat crop in 1936 still remain extremely doubtful. There has been no moisture of any kind since the light snow of early January. On a seventy-mile drive yesterday to arrange for hatchery chicks and to sell our week's cream and eggs, we saw more wheat that would still respond to immediate rainfall than I, with my stay-at-home habits, had expected to see. A few fields were refreshingly green and beautiful to look upon. There seems no doubt that improved methods of tillage and protection are already yielding some results in reducing wind erosion. But rain must come soon to encourage growth even on the best fields if there is to be any wheat harvest. Interspersed with the more hopeful areas are other tracts apparently abandoned to their fate. A field dotted thickly with shoulder-high hummocks of sand and soil bound together by the inevitable Russian thistles presents little encouragement to the most ardent conservationist. My own verdict in regard to plans for the reclaiming of such land would be, "Too late." Yet such fields are a menace to all the cultivated land or pasture ground around them and present a most difficult problem.

The two extremes I have just suggested—that is, the slight hope even yet for some production on carefully tilled fields, and the practically hopeless conditions on abandoned land—

are indicative of the two conflicting tendencies now evident through an extensive section of the High Plains. On the one hand we note a disposition to recognize a mistake, to turn aside from the undertaking with the least possible loss and direct one's time and energy to some new purpose. On the other hand we observe that many seem determined to use even the hard experiences of the past, their own mistakes and other people's, as warning signals, pointing the way to changes of method and more persistent and effective effort right where they stand.

The first attitude may be illustrated by an incident of the past week, the attempt of former neighbors to sell the pipe from the well on their now deserted homestead. This may not seem significant to you. But to old-timers in this deep-water country, so nearly destitute of flowing streams, the virtual destruction of a well of our excellent, life-nourishing water comes close to being the unpardonable sin against future generations.

The same disintegrating tendency is shown in a larger and more alarming way by the extent to which land once owned and occupied by farm families is now passing into ownership of banks, mortgage companies, assurance societies, and investment partnerships or corporations. The legal notices published in our county paper for the past week include two notices of foreclosure proceedings and nine notices of sheriff's sales to satisfy judgments previously rendered. These eleven legal actions involve the ownership of 3520 acres of land, the equivalent of twenty-two quarter sections, the original homestead allotment in this territory. In only two cases apparently had the loan been made from one person to another. Four life-insurance companies, one investment company, and one joint-stock land bank are included among the plaintiffs.

These forced sales take place just outside the window of the assessor's office, and we were told that they have now become merely a matter of routine. No one tries to redeem the property in question; no one even makes a bid on it; in fact, no one appears but the sheriff and the lawyer representing the plaintiff.

I am not questioning the legal right of these companies to take over the title of the farms for their own security or that of the people whose money they have invested. In a sense their action in pressing their claims may hold some encouragement for the rest of us, since it suggests that they look in time for a return of value to the acres which at present no one seeks to rescue. In addition to the large amount of land now owned by these corporate interests, very many farms belong to nonresident individuals. The "quarters" north and south of our own place are so held, while the one on the west has recently been taken over by an investment company. Unquestionably this remote control stands in the way of constructive efforts toward recovery.

Yet there are numerous evidences of the persevering restoration of which I have written. The big road maintainers keep the highways in excellent condition. New license tags are appearing on cars and trucks. Churches, schools, and basketball tournaments continue much as usual. One village church reported forty people in attendance on one of the darkest and most dangerous of the recent dusty Sundays. The state agricultural college for this section has an increased enrollment this year. More people are managing in some way—we hardly see how—to keep in touch with the world of news and markets, politics and entertainment, through radio service. A local implement agency recently sent out invitations to a tractor entertainment with free moving pictures of factory operation and the like. The five hundred free lunches prepared for the occasion proved insufficient for the assembled crowd. Within a few succeeding days the company took orders for three tractors ranging in price from around $1200 to $1500. Some people must still have faith in the future!

More impressive to me was the Saturday rush of activity at the small produce house where we did our marketing. Cars kept driving up and people coming in with pails or crates or cases of eggs. Cream was delivered in containers of all sorts and sizes, including one heavy aluminum cooker! Eggs were bringing fifteen cents per dozen and cream thirty cents a pound of tested butterfat. No large sums of money were involved. In many cases the payments were pitifully small, but every such sale represents hard work and economy and struggle to keep going. . . .

Our personal plans—like those of all the rest—are entirely dependent on whether or not rain comes to save a little of our wheat, to give grass or even weeds for pasturage, to permit the growing of roughage for the winter, and provide some cover on the surface and promote the intertwining of rootlets in the soil to reduce wind damage. Our terraces are in good condition to distribute whatever moisture may come. We hope we have learned a little about protecting the soil which is the basis of our physical life. In the house the poinsettia and Christmas cactus are blooming a second time and the geraniums blossom in spite of the dust. Eleanor has just sent us budded hyacinth and daffodil bulbs in little moss-filled nests. They will help us to look forward for a time at least.

CHAPTER 2

Who Were the "Okies"?

WHAT HAPPENED TO THOSE PEOPLE WHOSE FARMS—AS Mrs. Henderson reported—were turned over to the mortgage-holders at forced sales? The distinguished photographer Margaret Bourke-White reported in *The Nation* (May 22, 1935) that while taking pictures of the dust-beset areas she had passed on the road many families with all they owned packed on a wagon or, rarely, an old automobile. Where were they going?

Unlike many dispossessed tenant farmers from the deep South who migrated to large cities to vegetate, these proud and stubborn descendants of the pioneers were looking for work on an unspoiled frontier. As Mrs. Henderson observed in one of her letters, "We cannot complain of laziness on the part of our citizens. Oklahoma is one of the first states to get away from direct relief. Official reports . . . emphasize the eagerness with which people accept any sort of work to help themselves and to make unnecessary the acceptance of public aid."

To these people movement had traditionally meant opportunity—a land of plenty lay ahead for the taking. The migrants of the thirties, however, found the El Dorado beyond the mountains already occupied—as Steinbeck stresses —by those prepared to fight off interlopers with all the cunning and force at their disposal.

So the migrants became the hated "Okies." The pejorative term was applied not only to the many Oklahomans among the outcasts, but to all those from Texas and Kansas —anywhere in the Southwest or the northern plains—who had joined the trek into the sunset. "Okie" bore the same venomous connotation as "kike," "nigger," "wop"—any epithet applied to a minority group whose struggle for survival threatens the complacency of the majority. The "Okies" experienced all the humiliation and terror of belonging to such a despised minority in a time of crisis.

The plight of the "Okies" was described in an account published in *Fortune*, the opulently turned-out journal of American business, in 1939. Carefully assembled by the editors from on-the-scene observations, the article was illustrated both with magnificent Farm Security Administration photographs and with pastoral water colors by Millard Sheets. The glowing tones of the paintings contrast ironically with the harrowing details of the article, as though the magazine were seeking some way to lighten the dark blot on the American landscape. Another account of the "Okies" appeared the same year in *Factories in the Field*, a history and analysis of the migrant labor problem in California by Carey McWilliams, then Commissioner of Immigration and Housing of the State of California and the target, along with Steinbeck, of those whose exploitation of the desperate migrants he sought to expose. These two complementary accounts help us to understand what the term "Okie" meant in the troubled thirties.

The Editors of Fortune
"*I Wonder Where We Can Go Now*"

The migrants are familiar enough to anyone who has traveled much through California's interior. On the roads, where you can see them in numbers, they take on a kind of patchwork pattern. They come along in wheezy old cars with the father or one of the older boys driving. The mother and the younger children sit in back; and around them, crammed inside and overflowing to the running boards, the front and rear bumpers, the top and sides, they carry along everything they own. A galvanized iron washtub is tied to the rear, a dirty, patched tent lashed to a fender. There is a cast-iron stove, a mattress, some boxes full of old dishes, extra clothing, and a few staple groceries like flour, lard, and potatoes. You see, at odd angles, the protruding handle of a broom, part of a paint-flaked bedstead, perhaps even an old phonograph or radio. You notice the faces of the people in these cars. There is worry, but also something more: they are the faces of people afraid of hunger; completely dispossessed, certain only of being harried along when their immediate usefulness is over. . . . California's agricultural system could not exist without them—that is, without some of them. But there are far, far more of them than the system can utilize. Like certain of the state's home-grown products, they represent glut, depreciation, and decay.

They live under physical conditions ranging from the fairly tolerable to the terribly bad. Most of California's growers supply either tent space or permanent shelter on their own land, and it is noteworthy that they spent some $3,000,000 in the last two years, largely at the insistence of the Associated Farmers, a growers' pressure group of which more will be seen later. Some

From *Fortune*, XIX (April 1939), 90-94, 112-119, © 1939 Time Inc. Reprinted by special permission of *Fortune* magazine.

growers' camps are well built and equipped, but the average is poor. The last reports of the state Division of Immigration and Housing, which since 1933 has had only three full-time inspectors for the job of examining over eight thousand public and private camps, rate almost a third of them as "bad," i.e., either poorly equipped or poorly policed. . . . But not even the big growers provide housing for more than a part of their peak labor load. Many of the migrants live in dirty roadside tourist camps, labor contractors' camps, or privately run tenting grounds, where the rents may be as high or higher [than the $1 to $10 a month in the growers' camps] but the equipment is more primitive. Some live in squatter camps. Conditions in these shelters are notoriously squalid, particularly in the Imperial Valley, which offers the absolute low for the entire state. . . .*

Briefly and in its grimmest aspects, this is the tragedy in California. As a single state's problem of coping with an unwanted glut of humanity, it would warrant serious study. But it concerns us here in an even larger sense, i.e., as the most aggravated effect of a national situation—a situation so grave that President Roosevelt in February ordered an attack upon it by a committee headed by W.P.A. Administrator F. C. Harrington. California is generally supposed to harbor 150,000 to 250,000 of the estimated million-odd agricultural migrants including families in the United States—many more than any other state. But the most important reasons for that lie outside California's control. They lie specifically at the heart of the national migrant problem, and to understand them it is necessary to look across the plains with a long focus.

The migrations of distressed people are, of course, as old as history itself. When things look a little better somewhere else, men move on; the only static population is the population of

* There follows here a long report filed in 1936 by the Division of Special Surveys and Studies, State Relief Administration of California, which includes a detailed description of conditions in camps in the Imperial Valley substantially the same as that in Chapter 2 of Steinbeck's *Their Blood is Strong* (page 59).—ED.

the cemeteries. Movement, relocation, far from being deplorable, are in fact essential to an active economy, the demands of which can be compared to the pressure areas on a barometric map. Masses of workers shift like air currents from high- to low-pressure areas, but with a difference. The air currents obey physical laws, while the currents of foot-loose humanity, theoretically governed by the neat laws of classical economics, move too often on rumor, sentiment, hope, and malicious deception. . . .

There are two kinds of agricultural migrants. One group can be thought of as "habitual" migrants, which means that they have followed migratory life for years and will probably go on following it until they grow too old to work. The others are "removal" migrants, which means that they have been forced into migratory life by dispossession from land or job; most of them have been on the road only a few months or a few years, most of them are family units, and nearly all of them would settle permanently if they could.

The habitual migrants, mostly single men, are much the smaller group. Two years ago they were estimated conservatively at between 200,000 and 350,000, and there are probably as many today. . . . The habitual migrant, however underpaid, underfed, and underemployed, has the dignity of a way of life. It is even possible to think of him romantically. But there is no romance in the "removal" migrant families. They are the truly dispossessed, unequipped for the hazards of the road, searching only for a place to stop and take root.

Removal migrants have taken to the road from distressed areas all over the United States, but mostly from the South and Midwest. The causes of their distress are embedded deep in the whole tragic history of American agriculture, dating from the earliest misuse of the soil. The intervening chapters are familiar —land speculation, recurrent depressions and droughts, reduction of industrial outlets to surplus farm population, power farming, soil erosion, all leading up to the climax of the disastrous droughts and dust storms in the 1930s. With that final calamity, the thin stream of dispossessed families from the Great Plains states erupted in full force into a mass upheaval in 1934. Since then more than 200,000 persons have left the drought area, and others are leaving every day. Rains and federal aid have slowed the migration in some areas. But neither temporary rain nor government money can reverse the fact that large sections of the Great Plains cannot afford a decent living for even their present population. According to land economists, the minimum desirable amount of reconversion to grazing would probably displace another 250,000 to 400,000 people. If the pattern of the last few years can be taken as a guide, many of them would pile their family goods and kin into second-hand automobiles, set out with a few dollars, and drive west to join the overflowing stream of migratory farm workers.

Everybody knows about the so-called dust-bowl migration; its spectacular effects have made vivid copy in the press. But there has been another distress force at work, far more insidious yet potentially even more drastic: the spread of power farming. . . . A common procedure is for a landowner to throw several tenant-operated farms into one operating unit, evict the tenant families, and hire a tractor driver by the day. Usually it is impossible for the evicted tenant to get another place: he must go into the towns and live on relief, or hire himself out for whatever day labor the farms require, or move away and try for a new start somewhere else. Tens of thousands have already been displaced, and it is the sober conclusion of economists that if the present trend continues, a majority of the South's 1,800,000 tenants will be added to the nation's landless and jobless. If and when the mechanical cotton picker is finally perfected, these people will have not even the seasonal recourse of cotton picking.

It is an ironical sidelight that the government's crop-control program has abetted the dispossession. Crop restriction in itself reduces the labor need, and therefore causes some eviction.

But, more important, the benefit payments have furnished landowners with the capital to buy tractors. In addition, though the law requires that benefit checks be divided between owner and tenant, owners in many cases have secured the whole amount for themselves by dismissing the tenants and rehiring them as wage workers. The disturbances in southeastern Missouri last January, when some three hundred tenant-cropper families camped on the highways in public protest, were directed partly against this practice. But such isolated acts of treachery, however cruel, are merely incidental to the forces that are crowding the southern farm workers by the thousands off the land and into the army of migrants. . . .

To an outsider, with ideas about agriculture derived from the East or Middle West, the intensity of California agriculture is fairly visible. The "farms," particularly in the Imperial Valley, are more like big food factories, with every device of scientific farming used to secure maximum output from the soil. Instead of farmhouses with barns and outbuildings, there are mostly long rows of shacks along the ditch banks and in the eucalyptus groves. The "farmers" of much of the land are absentee owners, with offices in the cities, who do their farming through local managers. Even the managers are likely to live in town. The crops and terrain and acreages vary through the state, but the pattern of high-pressure land use prevails. California's agriculture is not "farming" in the traditional sense. It is industry as much as lumbering and oil are industries.

Figures make the point clear. In California today less than one-tenth of the farms produce more than one-half of the crops, while the small farmers (41.4 per cent) produce only 6 per cent. One-third of all United States large-scale farms (annual crop value of $30,000) are in California. The trend has been to corporate farming under absentee ownership, with a decrease in independent family-size farms.

To work these farms, with their violently fluctuating labor

demands, landowners in the past encouraged heavy immigration of low-wage workers from abroad—Chinese, Japanese, a few Hindus, thousands of Filipinos. More important than any of these races, however, were the Mexicans who began arriving in large numbers about 1910 and thereafter supplied the bulk of the migrant forces for two decades. . . . But through the immigration law, and also because the free-land policy of the Mexican government after 1934 attracted many back to their homeland, the Mexican migrants have become a much diminished force.

Throughout all these years there were, of course, some thousands of white native-born citizens among the migrants. A few traveled in family groups, but customarily they were single men, harvest followers of the kind who worked in the wheat harvests of the grain states. After 1930 the whole character of the California migrants began to change. Numbers of semi-urban unemployed Californians went into the fields to replace the departed Mexicans. Then single unemployed workers, both urban and rural, streamed into California from all over the country—a serious addition to the chronic oversupply. And finally, beginning in 1935, came the Dust Bowl hordes and the dispossessed southern tenants—far more than the farm economy could absorb—and an ordinary labor situation became an acute sociological problem.

Plant quarantine stations along the state's borders counted 285,000 refugees (including some duplications) "in need of manual employment" in the period from mid-1935 to January 1, 1939, besides 59,000 returning Californians of the same type. So alarming in size and suddenness was this mass migration that the Los Angeles Chamber of Commerce attempted briefly—and quite illegally—to shunt it aside by means of a "bum blockade" on main highways at the state borders. The total number of refugees since 1930 is unknown, but it may well reach 350,000. Naturally not all of these people have become migratory farm laborers; some have returned home, some have become resident laborers, a few have settled on small subsistence farms, and probably most of the pre-1935 single migrants have gone into the cities to join the ranks of the casually employed or unemployed. But the results so far as migrant farm labor is concerned are these: the racial characteristic has changed from predominantly foreign to predominantly white American, the single migrant has given way to the family group, and the number of migrants has swelled to an army that California agriculture cannot conceivably support.

The consequence of low income and privation is social unrest, and there is plenty of social unrest among California's migrants. But until recently there was surprisingly little articulate protest. On the surface, the situation would seem susceptible to union agitation, but it contains special elements: the migrants have no money to pay dues, and they move about so often and so far that it is difficult to weld them into a militant, closely knit group. Moreover, the traditional craft setup of American unionism offered no place to the unskilled worker, and consequently none to the farm laborer. The I.W.W. did heavy duty after 1913, the year of the bloody Wheatland hop riots, but fell apart in the early twenties. The A.F. of L. made several feeble attempts at organizing on a craft basis between 1909 and 1915, and again in the early thirties, but not much came of it. The Mexican and Filipino workers had their private organizations and occasionally caused the growers trouble. It remained for a Communist-led union, the Cannery and Agricultural Workers Industrial Union, to organize the first effective drive among the migrants.

This group appeared in California in 1930 but didn't get fully under way until 1933. In the spring and early summer of that year it followed the crops as they ripened, organizing in peas, lettuce, strawberries, and peaches, and having its most notable success in a nine-county cotton pickers' strike that affected 12,000 workers. By the middle of the 1934 working season, the union had led about fifty strikes involving some

50,000 workers. Its leaders claim that at its height it had a membership of around 21,000, and that it raised the basic hourly field wage from an average of 15 to 17.5 cents an hour in 1932 to an average of 27.5 cents in 1934. In the summer of 1934, however, the union was broken up by the anti-Red activities of employers and state authorities. Its last stand was an apricot pickers' strike in June 1934, on the Balfour, Guthrie ranches near Brentwood.* Deputies herded two hundred strikers into a cattle pen, arrested some of their leaders, and convoyed the rest out of the county. In the trials following the big California Red scare of 1934, the union's president and secretary, along with six of their associates, were convicted of treason under the criminal-syndicalism law. Five of the eight prisoners were later paroled and the remaining three were liberated when an appellate court reversed all the convictions in 1937.

After the demise of the C.&A.W.I.U., the Communist party in California gave most of its attention to the industrial situation in San Francisco. Now, however, it is understood to be concentrating again on agricultural workers. The international party "line" changed in 1934 from a tactic of parallel unionism to one of united-front collaboration, so the Communists work through the C.I.O.'s United Cannery, Agricultural, Packing, and Allied Workers of America, which was formed in 1937. This new group has the arena pretty much to itself, since the A.F. of L. has preferred to give most of its time to the canneries, where the packers have welcomed it as a bulwark against the hated C.I.O. Possibly because so much of its energy has been drawn off in the cannery battle, the C.I.O. has not made an impressive showing among the field and shed workers, claiming only 5000 of them in the California district. It has led nine of the fourteen field workers' strikes of the last year and a half (employers charge the union with instigation; the union says the

---

* Steinbeck's *In Dubious Battle* was not modeled upon this or any other single strike, but was a composite picture drawn from all the strikes of this period.—ED.

strikes were spontaneous). Eight of the nine union-led strikes ended in union victory or compromise.

Though the union's membership is small its mere existence as strike threat fills California's growers with panic. Harvesting can't wait on negotiation. Crops must be picked within a few days of ripening or not at all; and if not at all, the result may be financial ruin. This has created a situation of which thoughtful Californians are far from proud. Vigilante activity against strikers and organizers since 1932 has been bloody and direct. Scores of workers have been injured and so have a number of strikebreakers and deputized townspeople and farmers. California's industrialized farming can exhibit all the customary weapons of industrial warfare including tear gas, finks, goon squads, propaganda, bribery, and espionage.

Spearhead of the growers in this unhappy situation is the Associated Farmers. Composed mainly of small or medium-scale farm operators, this organization is dominated by the big growers, packers, utilities, banks, and other absentee landlords who are all-important in the state's farm system. Now the A.F.'s stated objectives are thoroughly worthy. And it will be recalled that A.F. engineered the growers' expenditure of $3,-000,000 to improve the housing of migrants. But its tactics in labor disputes are infinitely less enlightened. It claims to be "not anti-union or anti-labor," but it takes pride in having helped enact antipicketing ordinances in the majority of California's fifty-eight counties. A.F. members were in the thick of the worst recent strikes. In the particularly bloody Salinas lettuce strike, the county head of the A.F. himself convoyed the lettuce trucks and led the battle against the strikers. In the Stockton cannery strike, it was the organization's Pacific Coast president who brought in a thousand deputized farmers to see that the spinach was canned. From labor's point of view, the Associated Farmers is a thinly camouflaged strikebreaking agency. To the big grower, it is a strong-arm defense against the menace of Communist agitation. The small grower's view is less clear-cut, but he often finds it healthier to join the Associated Farmers than not, if he wants to get crop loans from the banks. Incidentally, investigation of the A.F. was next on the docket of the La Follette Civil Liberties Committee when that body was allowed to expire last January.

Vigilantism is an alarming and dangerous thing in a democracy, but it is not uncommon. It is, in fact, a characteristic of industrial warfare whether the locale be Michigan, Pennsylvania, or Mohawk Valley. But California's worker-grower relationship contains something more than physical violence. On the side of the growers it often contains an antipathy amounting almost to hatred, and this may seem odd in view of the fact that the growers could not exist without the aid of the migrants. The reasons are of two kinds, one emotional, the other economic. The first kind can be summed up in a composite grower statement—with many exceptions among individuals, of course—that runs about like this:

"We didn't ask these Okies and Arkies to come out here. They were failures where they lived, and they came because our relief payments are about the biggest in the country. Most of them aren't the kind of people who make good citizens. They're naturally dirty, ignorant, immoral, and superstitious. If you do anything for them they don't appreciate it, and if you let them on your ground they dirty it up and destroy property—they're used to living like trash. They've been inbreeding for so long that they're low-grade stock. After they've been here a year or two and learned how to handle our crops they make good workers, maybe the best we've ever had, but you can't depend on them. They're too damned independent; they won't take orders like a Mexican or a Jap, and they're not satisfied with the wages we can afford to pay. They're easy bait for the Red organizers. They're not satisfied with what they have, and yet if you gave them a hundred-acre farm and all the equipment they'd go bankrupt again inside of five years."

There is some fact in this view, but a great deal more fiction.

From experienced sociologists who have worked among the migrants (Dr. Paul S. Taylor of the University of California is one of the most eminent authorities in the United States on agricultural migrant labor) and from *Fortune*'s own observation a more accurate general statement would be this:

"The majority of the migrants are ordinary Americans who have been dispossessed mostly by forces outside their control. Most of them are unskilled farm laborers, though there are workmen and tradespeople among them—mechanics, construction workers, miners, salesmen, and so on. They haven't had much schooling but they are intelligent enough. They are anxious to work and they don't like to take relief. They appreciate what is done for them. They are mildly religious, their moral standards are fair. Their standards of cleanliness are normal under decent conditions, but they tend to succumb to the effects of squalid surroundings. They are standoffish, and they don't work well together. Some of them have become so far demoralized by long unemployment and substandard living that possibly they can never be rehabilitated; they have even lost ambition. But for the most part they are potentially self-supporting citizens who want only a chance to make a new start."

That, then, is the emotional argument over the migrant. In the economic argument the growers have better reason for short tempers. It is imperative that the growers have enough mobile labor to meet their peak seasonal demand of some 175,000 workers, but afterward many of that number become sheer surplus, and the growers feel no more obligation toward them than a New York department-store owner, for example, might feel toward part-time clerks laid off after a rush season. While they acknowledge their dependence upon the 175,000, growers nevertheless argue that an employer cannot be held responsible for the year-round maintenance of workers needed only for a few weeks or months. And since agriculture supplies a considerable share of California's productive wealth, some believe it reasonable that the workers be subsidized during slack seasons by relief payments—but no relief to the uninvited surplus workers. Furthermore, as the growers vehemently point out, California's farm-labor wage rates are among the highest in the nation. If it were possible to give the migrants steady work their incomes would be above national average for unskilled labor. Obviously steady work is impossible because: (1) the work is seasonal, (2) jobs are widely separated and time must be lost on the road, and (3) lacking accurate information, migrants move about on hope and rumor, with a consequent inefficient distribution of workers to available jobs.

Carey McWilliams
The End of a Cycle

In 1937 it became increasingly apparent that a basic change had taken place in the character of farm labor in California. Although the change had been taking place for some time, it was suddenly realized in 1937 that the bulk of the state's migratory workers were white Americans and that the foreign racial groups were no longer a dominant factor. The change had, in fact, commenced about 1933, at the bottom of the Depression. At the end of 1934 the Commission of Immigration and Housing estimated that roughly fifty per cent of the labor-camp population was native white American, with about one-third Mexican and the balance made up of Filipinos (eleven per cent), Japanese (three per cent), and Chinese (three per cent). The first reaction to this discovery was rather naïve: "Our Race Problems Vanish," editorialized the *San Francisco News,* pointing out that the possibility of a "permanently stratified society in

From *Factories in the Field,* by Carey McWilliams (Boston: Little, Brown, 1939), copyright 1935, 1939 by Carey McWilliams. Portions of Chapter 17 (pp. 305-325) are reprinted here by permission of the author.

California" would probably cease with the elimination of the minority racial groups. But the pattern of exploitation has not been altered; it remains exactly the same. The established pattern has been somewhat as follows: to bring in successive minority groups; to exploit them until the advantages of exploitation have been exhausted; and then to expel them in favor of more readily exploitable material. In this manner the Chinese, the Japanese, the Filipinos, and the Mexicans have, as it were, been run through the hopper. From what source, then, was the latest army being recruited? The answer was soon forthcoming: from the stricken dust-bowl areas, from Oklahoma, Texas, Arkansas. The new recruits were refugees from drought and disaster. The circumstances of their misery made them admirable recruits. They came in without expense to the growers; they were excellent workers; they brought their families; they were so impoverished that they would work for whatever wage was offered. They came, moreover, in great numbers. The growers naturally seized upon these workers as a providential dispensation. But they failed to perceive that, with the arrival of the dust-bowl refugees, a cycle of exploitation had been brought to a close. These despised "Okies" and "Texicans" were not another minority alien racial group (although they were treated as such) but American citizens familiar with the usages of democracy. With the arrival of the dust-bowl refugees a day of reckoning approaches for the California farm industrialists. The jig, in other words, is about up.

The first consideration to be kept in mind is that the influx of dust-bowl refugees differs qualitatively and quantitatively from previous migrations. [Earlier] the California growers themselves set in motion the currents of migratory labor: first, by expropriating the small settlers and squatters; second, by deliberately encouraging and soliciting "tourist" emigration through the activities of the California Development Association and similar organizations; third, by recruiting, particularly in the nineties, out-of-state workers; and, fourth, by fostering the

"Dirty Plate Route" along which the tramps, bindle stiffs, bums, and hoboes of former years used to plod their way on foot and by freight cars. In fact, the tramp as such, the authentic hobo of California tradition, has never passed out of existence. Another refinement must be noted: the professional "fruit tramp" still exists. Mr. William Plunkert, in an admirable social document, has traced the life history of a family which has "followed the crops" in California for twenty-four years. It should be pointed out, also, that families from Texas and Oklahoma appeared in the valleys as early as 1921, primarily as cotton pickers.

But the migration which began in 1933, and which rapidly increased throughout 1934, 1935, 1936, and 1937, has been of an entirely different character. The presence of these latter-day emigrants was not altogether solicited (although many of them say that they had read advertisements for work in California); they came like grasshoppers driven before a storm. They have come, moreover, in such numbers as to constitute a major migration somewhat comparable to the great influx of '49. During the year 1935-1936, 87,302 migratory workers entered California, of whom nine-tenths were white persons and over a third were from Oklahoma, Texas, and Arkansas. It has been estimated that a total of 221,000 have entered the state since 1933 (the Farm Security Administration, on April 5, 1938, announced that it was attempting to provide for 45,500 destitute dust-bowl refugees in California who had been "burned out, blown out, eaten out"). On November 20, 1937, 3000 pea pickers entered the Imperial Valley from Arizona. The caravan of cars made up four lines of traffic along the highway, with as many as thirteen people to the car, the largest single influx of its kind ever noted by local authorities. *Business Week* for July 3, 1937, estimated that 30,000 *families* had entered California from the dust bowl and aptly characterized this shift in population as "one of the greatest inter-state migrations since the gold rush."

"This," commented the *Pacific Rural Press* for May 22, 1937, "is not a bindle-stiff movement."

The acute social problem presented by this amazing emigration was soon accentuated by other factors. On September 20, 1935, the Federal Emergency Relief Administration ordered the liquidation of the Federal Transient Service, which had, at one time, provided relief for 38,815 transients in California: 13.5 per cent of all transients in the country. With the abrupt discontinuance of federal assistance, the local authorities became wildly hysterical. The methods by which they have ever since attempted to cope with the problem have been, to say the least, curious. The first step in this direction was the creation of the Los Angeles Committee on Indigent Alien Transients, headed by James E. Davis, Chief of Police. In flat disregard of constitutional provisions, this power-drunk functionary of the Los Angeles Chamber of Commerce proceeded to establish some sixteen border patrols staffed by the Los Angeles City Police, the patrols being located in counties hundreds of miles removed from Los Angeles. Throughout November and December 1935, and January, February, March, and April 1936, some 125 policemen stationed at these various points of entry stopped all cars that looked as though they might contain "unemployables" and turned them back. When a court action was brought in the United States District Court by the American Civil Liberties Union, to test the constitutionality of this procedure, the chief of police detailed the head of his celebrated "Intelligence Squad" to "work over" the plaintiff in whose name the action had been commenced. Not only was the plaintiff himself intimidated, but his wife and child were threatened and browbeaten by police officers (one of whom has since been convicted in Los Angeles of attempted murder); and, ultimately, the plaintiff was "induced" to drop the action. The patrol unquestionably checked the influx of refugees, but the effect of the blockade was to "back up" the refugees and temporarily delay their entry into

California. Repercussions of the blockade were felt as far East as El Paso (see *Monthly Labor Review,* December 1936).

Recourse was had to other time-honored stratagems to stem the tide of migrants. A bill was introduced in the Legislature to bar all transients from the state; stiff vagrancy sentences were given "alien transients"; transients failing to meet the three-years residence requirement for relief were left to starve; many were rounded up by the relief officials and shipped out of the state; and, in the rural counties, transients were shifted back and forth from one county to the other, in the vain and foolish hope that somehow, in this elaborate reshuffling process, they would suddenly disappear. By these and other methods, the influx was somewhat checked (the border patrol was, for example, given wide publicity in the Middle West); but the transient problem remained. Nothing was done, of course, to settle the matter and the transients were left to fend for themselves. An obliging people, they continued to starve until a series of major revelations focused public attention on a problem that could no longer be ignored. (See "Towards a National Policy for Migration," by Eric Beecroft and Seymour Janow, *Social Forces,* May 1938; and "Labor on Wheels," by Frank J. Taylor, *Country Gentleman,* July 1938.)

The first revelation to attract widespread attention had to do with 2000 pea pickers marooned in Nipomo, a small community north of Santa Barbara. For two preceding seasons, labor contractors, licensed by the state of California, had been permitted to advertise in Arizona newspapers for "thousands" of pea pickers, promising work "for the season." In response to these appeals, 2000 workers had assembled at Nipomo in the spring of 1937 only to discover, of course, that there was work for but a third of their number. To complicate matters, rain destroyed a portion of the crop and flooded the camp of the workers. Those who had any funds at all moved on; some sold what belongings they had and tried to escape. But about 2000, trapped in their miserable camp, were actually starving when a representative of the Federal Surplus Commodities Corporation discovered their plight. Local authorities admitted that there was "some distress" but tried to duck responsibility. Federal agencies rushed in supplies of food and medicine, and managed to help the workers along until the other crops matured. The pictures taken at this camp, by federal representatives, are almost incredible in their revelation of the plight of 2000 starving, dirty, utterly dejected men, women, and children. I know of nothing comparable to these pictures except the scenes of the famine areas in postwar Europe. But irony must be added to misery in order to complete the picture. When the pea pickers who remained in the camp until the storms were over and the picking started attempted to strike on April 15, 1937, for decent wages, the local sheriff told them to go to work or leave the county or face arrest on vagrancy charges. To back up this ultimatum, he proceeded to swear in over a hundred special deputy sheriffs. Needless to say, there was no strike.

A bad situation, indeed; but precisely the same tragedy occurred in the spring of 1938. On March 11, 1938, the press announced that six hundred families were again stranded at Nipomo, where labor contractors for the third year had overestimated the number of workers required.

In July, 1937, Californians were shocked by a sensational address by Mr. Harold Robertson, national field secretary of the Gospel Army, who charged that 70,000 transients were starving in the great valley of the San Joaquin. Speaking from personal observation, Mr. Robertson announced that "people are seeking shelter and subsistence in the fields and woods like wild animals" and that children were working in the cotton fields for fifteen cents and twenty cents a day. Lured to the valley by announcements that 25,000 additional workers were required to harvest the 1937 cotton crop, a vast army of transients had assembled there to starve. Under the impetus of this forceful address, the social agencies got busy and conducted an investigation which amply confirmed the charges. The situation was tided over, for the time being, when the Farm Security Administration assumed the burden of supporting the transients. But the problem has not been solved; it has merely been shoved forward. And the army of transients continues to camp in the San Joaquin.

The investigations of 1937 [conducted by the State Relief Administration] revealed that migratory workers were receiving incredibly low wages. Dr. Omer Mills found wages in the cotton district to be as low as fifty cents a day and that they were tending to decrease; he also found that some workers were making $2 and $3 a week and were attempting to support families on these earnings. Dr. Paul Taylor estimates the average annual income for migratory workers at between $350 and $400. The State Relief Administration estimates that most agricultural workers only have employment for six months in the year or less; and that the average yearly earnings per family group dropped from $381 in 1930 to $289 in 1935. In the same study, the S.R.A. estimated that each family, in 1935, should have had at least $780 to eke out an existence. The average period of employment for migratory workers is nowhere more than thirty weeks a year. In the summer of 1937, during the height of the harvest season, 6000 migratory workers applied for relief in the San Joaquin valley alone. In 1932 there were 181 agricultural workers for every 100 jobs offered; in 1933, 185; and for the first seven months of 1934, 142. The same report indicates 60,000 unemployed agricultural workers as of April 1935, in the face of the growers' insistence that an "acute labor shortage" existed.

Most of the investigators agree that the new migrants, the dust-bowl refugees, are here to stay. Mr. Ray Zeman estimated that at least 95 per cent of the transients who had come to California from the dust bowl had no intention of returning: "They are mobile only in following the seasonal work north and south in the valley." Most of them lost their residence in the states from which they fled and are determined to acquire legal residence in California. The prejudice against the migratory worker has always been intense, white migratory workers being treated in exactly the same manner as their predecessors, the Mexicans and the Japanese. As most of the migrants have not acquired legal residence, and therefore cannot vote, they can be discriminated against with political immunity. The "Okies" and the "Texicans" are looked down upon by the Californians and this curious condescension is reflected by the local official-dom. Mrs. Joan Pratt, county welfare department director in Tulare County, complains, "You can't change the habits of primitive people from the Southern and Middle Western states. You can't force them to bathe or to eat vegetables." A local police officer gives his view: "A shiftless stock and inclined to petty thievery and shirking of work." The field investigators, however, are unanimous in reporting that the dust-bowl refugees are orderly, neighborly—a patient and kindly folk—and that they "quickly assimilate new habits."

CHAPTER // 3

What Did John Steinbeck Know about the "Okies"?

ALTHOUGH BOOKS SUCH AS STEPHEN CRANE'S *The Red Badge of Courage* demonstrate that a novelist can write a memorable story without having first-hand experience of his subject, readers expect the writer who seeks to expose the evils of contemporary society to be able to say with Walt Whitman, "I am the man, I suffer'd, I was there."

John Steinbeck could claim such direct acquaintance with the plight of the Okies. The publication in 1936 of *In Dubious Battle* had established him as the literary voice of the California migrants—as well as the gadfly of the delinquent American conscience. His depiction of Communist tactics in that bitter novel had led to objections from leftist critics in New York; but Steinbeck told his agents (according to Lewis Gannett in the Introduction to *The Portable Steinbeck*) that he had acquired his information from Italian and Irish Communist organizers whose training was "in the field, not in the drawing-room."

When the then new picture magazine *Life* asked him to do an article about the migrants, he refused, because he did not feel he could "cash in" on the misery of these people. He did, however, write a series of stories, published in the *San Francisco News* between October 5 and 12, 1936, based on his observation of conditions in squatters' camps near his home town of Salinas, California, and near Bakersfield, a trading center in the San Joaquin Valley.

In the autumn of 1937, Steinbeck followed the trail of the migrants from Oklahoma to California, and lived with them in their roadside camps. On the basis of this experience, he wrote an epilogue to his 1936 newspaper reports, bringing them up to date, and they were published in 1938 as an illustrated pamphlet entitled *Their Blood Is Strong,* issued under the sponsorship of the Simon J. Lubin Society of California. Named for the late Simon Julius Lubin (1876-1936), a Sacramento businessman who was the founder and first head of the California State Commission of Immigration and Housing, the Lubin Society sought, with the backing of Governor Culbert L. Olson and other California political and social leaders, "to educate public opinion to an understanding of the problems of the working farmer and the condition of agricultural laborers, and the need of them both for progressive organization to better their conditions."

When World War II distracted attention from the migrants, the twenty-five-cent pamphlet went out of print; *Their Blood Is Strong* has since been difficult to locate and is little known even among Steinbeck's admirers. The complete text, reprinted in the following pages, is thus made generally available for the first time.

Readers of *The Grapes of Wrath* will recognize in the reports collected in *Their Blood Is Strong* many details which Steinbeck subsequently put to artistic use. It cannot be too strongly emphasized, however, that the novel does not merely duplicate the pamphlet. The earlier work is one of the author's few tracts. His attitude toward the matters he discusses, particularly his ideas about what might be done to solve the immediate problems of the migrants, are made far more explicit in the newspaper stories than in *The Grapes of Wrath*. Those who have complained that Steinbeck provides no "solutions" for the problems he depicts in the novel should read these articles carefully.

Not only does the pamphlet serve as an illustration of Steinbeck's ideas, it offers evidence, by contrast, that the novel is art rather than propaganda. Where the two works differ in tone, and in their treatment of the material, one can see that the changes were dictated by Steinbeck's effort to make his novel something *more* than a tract about an immediate situation: he was trying to present an enduring and crucial problem in human relations that stemmed from "man's inhumanity to man," but that happened to be epitomized by the situation of the migrants in California. *Their Blood Is Strong* provides information about a tragic episode in our history; it also serves as an illustration of the vast changes that occur when history is transmuted into art.

John Steinbeck
Their Blood Is Strong

1. THE PEOPLE, WHO THEY ARE

At the season of the year when California's great crops are coming into harvest, the heavy grapes, the prunes, the apples and lettuce and the rapidly maturing cotton, our highways swarm with the migrant workers, that shifting group of nomadic, poverty-stricken harvesters, driven by hunger and the threat of hunger from crop to crop, from harvest to harvest, up and down

The complete text of *Their Blood Is Strong* by John Steinbeck (San Francisco: The Simon J. Lubin Society of California, Inc., 1938) is reprinted here by permission of the author.

the state and into Oregon to some extent, and into Washington a little. But it is California which has and needs the majority of these workers. There are at least 150,000 homeless migrants wandering up and down the state, and that is an army large enough to make it important to every person in the state.

To the casual traveler on the great highways the movements of the migrants are mysterious if they are seen at all, for suddenly the roads will be filled with open rattletrap cars loaded with children and with dirty bedding, with fire-blackened cooking utensils. The boxcars and gondolas on the railroad lines will be filled with men. And then, just as suddenly, they will have disappeared from the main routes. On side roads and near rivers where there is little travel the squalid, filthy squatters' camp will have been set up, and the orchards will be filled with pickers and cutters and driers.

The unique nature of California agriculture requires that these migrants exist, and requires that they move about. Peaches and grapes, hops and cotton cannot be harvested by a resident population of laborers. For example, a large peach orchard which requires the work of twenty men the year round will need as many as 2000 for the brief time of picking and packing. And if the migration of the 2000 should not occur, if it should be delayed even a week, the crop will rot and be lost.

Thus, in California we find a curious attitude toward a group that makes our agriculture successful. The migrants are needed, and they are hated. Arriving in a district they find the dislike always meted out by the resident to the foreigner, the outlander. This hatred of the stranger occurs in the whole range of human history, from the most primitive village farm to our own highly organized industrial farming. The migrants are hated for the following reasons, that they are ignorant and dirty people, that they are carriers of disease, that they increase the necessity for police and the tax bill for schooling in a community, and that if they are allowed to organize they can, simply by refusing to work, wipe out the season's crops. They are never received into a community nor into the life of a community. Wanderers in fact, they are never allowed to feel at home in the communities that demand their services.

Let us see what kind of people they are, where they come from, and the routes of their wanderings. In the past they have been of several races, encouraged to come and often imported as cheap labor; Chinese in the early period, then Filipinos, Japanese, and Mexicans. These were foreigners, and as such they were ostracized and segregated and herded about.

If they attempted to organize they were deported or arrested, and having no advocates they were never able to get a hearing for their problems. But in recent years the foreign migrants have begun to organize, and at this danger signal they have been deported in great numbers, for there was a new reservoir from which a great quantity of cheap labor could be obtained.

The drought in the Middle West has driven the agricultural populations of Oklahoma, Nebraska, and parts of Kansas and Texas westward. Their lands are destroyed and they can never go back to them.

Thousands of them are crossing the borders in ancient rattling automobiles, destitute and hungry and homeless, ready to accept any pay so that they may eat and feed their children. And this is a new thing in migrant labor, for the foreign workers were usually imported without their children and everything that remains of their old life with them.

They arrive in California usually having used up every resource to get here, even to the selling of the poor blankets and utensils and tools on the way to buy gasoline. They arrive bewildered and beaten and usually in a state of semi-starvation, with only one necessity to face immediately, and that is to find work at any wage in order that the family may eat.

And there is only one field in California that can receive them. Ineligible for relief, they must become migratory field workers.

Because the old kind of laborers, Mexicans and Filipinos, are being deported and repatriated very rapidly, while on the other hand the river [of] dust-bowl refugees increases all the time, it is this new kind of migrant that we must largely consider.

The earlier foreign migrants have invariably been drawn from a peon class. This is not the case with the new migrants.

They are small farmers who have lost their farms, or farm hands who lived with the family in the old American way. They are men who have worked hard on their own farms and have felt the pride of possessing and living in close touch with the land.

They are resourceful and intelligent Americans who have gone through the hell of the drought, have seen their lands wither and die and the topsoil blow away; and this, to a man who has owned his land, is a curious and terrible pain.

And then they have made the crossing and have seen often the death of their children on the way. Their cars have broken down and been repaired with the ingenuity of the land man.

Often they patched the worn-out tires every few miles. They have weathered the thing, and they can weather much more for their blood is strong.

They are descendants of men who crossed into the Middle West, who won their lands by fighting, who cultivated the prairies and stayed with them until they went back to desert.

And because of their tradition and their training, they are not migrants by nature. They are gypsies by force of circumstance.

In their heads, as they move wearily from harvest to harvest, there is one urge and one overwhelming need, to acquire a little land again, and to settle on it and stop their wandering. One has only to go into the squatters' camps where the families live on the ground and have no homes, no beds, and no equipment; and one has only to look at the strong purposeful faces, often filled with pain and more often, when they see the corporation-held idle lands, filled with anger, to know that this new race is here to stay and that heed must be taken of it.

It should be understood that with this new race the old methods of repression, of starvation wages, of jailing, beating, and intimidation are not going to work; these are American people. Consequently we must meet them with understanding and attempt to work out the problem to their benefit as well as ours.

It is difficult to believe what one large speculative farmer has said, that the success of California agriculture requires that we create and maintain a peon class. For if this is true, then California must depart from the semblance of democratic government that remains here.

The names of the new migrants indicate that they are of English, German and Scandinavian descent. There are Munns, Holbrooks, Hansens, Schmidts.

And they are strangely anachronistic in one way: having been brought up in the prairies where industrialization never penetrated, they have jumped with no transition from the old agrarian, self-containing farm, where nearly everything used was raised or manufactured, to a system of agriculture so industrialized that the man who plants a crop does not often see, let alone harvest, the fruit of his planting, where the migrant has no contact with the growing cycle.

And there is another difference between their [old] life and the new. They have come from little farm districts where democracy was not only possible, but inevitable, where popular government, whether practiced in the Grange, in church organization, or in local government, was the responsibility of every man. And they have come into the country where, because of the movement necessary to make a living, they are not allowed any vote whatever, but are rather considered a properly underprivileged class.

Let us see the fields that require the impact of their labor and the districts to which they must travel. As one little boy in a squatters' camp said, "When they need us they call us migrants, and when we've picked their crop, we're bums and we got to get out."

There are the vegetable crops of the Imperial Valley, the lettuce, cauliflower, tomatoes, cabbage to be picked and packed, to be hoed and irrigated. There are several crops a year to be harvested, but there is not time distribution sufficient to give the migrants permanent work.

The orange orchards deliver two crops a year, but the picking season is short. Farther north, in Kern County and up the San Joaquin Valley, the migrants are needed for grapes, cotton, pears, melons, beans, and peaches.

In the outer valley, near Salinas, Watsonville, and Santa Clara there are lettuce, cauliflowers, artichokes, apples, prunes, apricots. North of San Francisco the produce is of grapes, deciduous fruits, and hops. The Sacramento Valley needs masses of migrants for its asparagus, its walnuts, peaches, prunes, and so on. These great valleys with their intensive farming make their seasonal demands on migrant labor.

A short time, then, before the actual picking begins, there is the scurrying on the highways, the families in open cars hurrying to the ready crops and hurrying to be first at work. For it has been the habit of the growers' associations of the state to provide, by importation, twice as much labor as was necessary, so that wages might remain low.

Hence the hurry, for if the migrant is a little late the places will be filled and he will have taken his trip for nothing. And there are many things that may happen even if he is in time. The crop may be late, or there may occur one of those situations like that at Nipomo last year when 1200 workers arrived to pick the pea crop only to find it spoiled by rain.

All resources having been used to get to the field, the migrants could not move on; they stayed and starved until government aid tardily was found for them.

And so they move, frantically, with starvation close behind them. And in this pamphlet we shall try to see how they live and what kind of people they are, what their living standard is, what is done for them and to them, and what their problems and needs are. For while California has been successful in its use of migrant labor, it is gradually building a human structure which will certainly change the state, and may, if handled with the inhumanity and stupidity that have characterized the past, destroy the present system of agricultural economics.

2. SQUATTERS' CAMPS

The squatters' camps are located all over California. Let us see what a typical one is like. It is located on the banks of a river, near an irrigation ditch or on a side road where a spring of water is available. From a distance it looks like a city dump, and well it may, for the city dumps are the sources of material of which it is built. You can see a litter of dirty rags and scrap iron, of houses built of weeds, of flattened cans or of paper. It is only on close approach that it can be seen that these are homes.

Here is a house built by a family who have tried to maintain a neatness. The house is about ten feet by ten feet, and it is built completely of corrugated paper. The roof is peaked, the walls are tacked to a wooden frame. The dirt floor is swept clean, and along the irrigation ditch or in the muddy river the wife of the family scrubs clothes without soap and tries to rinse out the mud in muddy water. The spirit of this family is not quite broken, for the children, three of them, still have clothes, and the family possesses three old quilts and a soggy, lumpy mattress. But the money so needed for food cannot be used for soap nor for clothes.

With the first rain the carefully built house will slop down into a brown, pulpy mush; in a few months the clothes will fray off the children's bodies, while the lack of nourishing food will subject the whole family to pneumonia when the first cold comes.

Five years ago this family had fifty acres of land and a thousand dollars in the bank. The wife belonged to a sewing circle and the man was a member of the Grange. They raised chickens, pigs, pigeons and vegetables and fruit for their own use; and their land produced the tall corn of the Middle West. Now they have nothing.

If the husband hits every harvest without delay and works the maximum time, he may make $400 this year. But if anything happens, if his old car breaks down, if he is late and misses a harvest or two, he will have to feed his whole family on as little as $150.

But there is still pride in this family. Wherever they stop they try to put the children in school. It may be that the children will be in a school for as much as a month before they are moved to another locality.

Here, in the faces of the husband and his wife, you begin to see an expression you will notice on every face, not worry, but absolute terror of the starvation that crowds in against the borders of the camp. This man has tried to make a toilet by digging a hole in the ground near his paper house and surrounding it with an old piece of burlap. But he will only do things like that this year.

He is a newcomer and his spirit and his decency and his sense of his own dignity have not been quite wiped out. Next year he will be like his next-door neighbor.

This is a family of six; a man, his wife and four children. They live in a tent the color of the ground. Rot has set in on the canvas so that the flaps and the sides hang in tatters and are held together with bits of rusty baling wire. There is one bed in the family, and that is a big tick lying on the ground inside the tent.

They have one quilt and a piece of canvas for bedding. The sleeping arrangement is clever. Mother and father lie down together and two children lie between them. Then, heading the other way, the other two children lie, the littler ones. If the mother and father sleep with their legs spread wide, there is room for the legs of the children.

There is more filth here. The tent is full of flies clinging to the apple box that is the dinner table, buzzing about the foul clothes of the children, particularly the baby, who has not been bathed nor cleaned for several days.

This family has been on the road longer than the builder of the paper house. There is no toilet here, but there is a clump of willows nearby where human faeces lie exposed to the flies— the same flies that are in the tent.

Two weeks ago there was another child, a four-year-old boy. For a few weeks they had noticed that he was kind of lackadaisical, that his eyes had been feverish.

They had given him the best place in the bed, between father and mother. But one night he went into convulsions and died, and the next morning the coroner's wagon took him away. It was one step down.

They knew pretty well that it was a diet of fresh fruit, beans, and little else that caused his death. He had had no milk for months. With this death there came a change of mind in this family. The father and mother now feel that paralyzed dullness with which the mind protects itself against too much sorrow and too much pain.

And this father will not be able to make a maximum of $400 a year any more because he is no longer alert; he isn't quick at piece-work, and he is not able to fight clear of the dullness that has settled on him. His spirit is losing caste rapidly.

The dullness shows in the faces of this family, and in addition there is a sullenness that makes them taciturn. Sometimes they still start the older children off to school, but the ragged little things will not go; they hide themselves in ditches or wander off by themselves until it is time to go back to the tent, because they are scorned in the school.

The better-dressed children shout and jeer, the teachers are quite often impatient with these additions to their duties, and the parents of the "nice" children do not want to have disease carriers in the schools.

The father of this family once had a little grocery store and his family lived in back of it so that even the children could wait on the counter. When the drought set in there was no trade for the store any more.

This is the middle class of the squatters' camp. In a few months this family will slip down to the lower class.

Dignity is all gone, and spirit has turned to sullen anger before it dies.

The next-door neighbor family, of man, wife, and three children of from three to nine years of age, have built a house by driving willow branches into the ground and wattling weeds, tin, old paper, and strips of carpet against them.

A few branches are placed over the top to keep out the noonday sun. It would not turn water at all. There is no bed.

Somewhere the family has found a big piece of old carpet. It is on the ground. To go to bed the members of the family lie on the ground and fold the carpet up over them.

The three-year-old child has a gunny sack tied about his middle for clothing. He has the swollen belly caused by malnutrition.

He sits on the ground in the sun in front of the house, and the little black fruit flies buzz in circles and land on his closed eyes and crawl up his nose until he weakly brushes them away.

They try to get at the mucus in the eye-corners. This child seems to have the reactions of a baby much younger. The first year he had a little milk, but he has had none since.

He will die in a very short time. The older children may survive. Four nights ago the mother had a baby in the tent, on the dirty carpet. It was born dead, which was just as well because she could not have fed it at the breast; her own diet will not produce milk.

After it was born and she had seen that it was dead, the mother rolled over and lay still for two days. She is up today, tottering around. The last baby, born less than a year ago, lived a week. This woman's eyes have the glazed, faraway look of a sleepwalker's eyes.

She does not wash clothes any more. The drive that makes for cleanliness has been drained out of her and she hasn't the energy. The husband was a share-cropper once, but he couldn't make it go. Now he has lost even the desire to talk.

He will not look directly at you, for that requires will, and will needs strength. He is a bad field worker for the same reason. It takes him a long time to make up his mind, so he is always late in moving and late in arriving in the fields. His top wage, when he can find work now, which isn't often, is a dollar a day.

The children do not even go to the willow clump any more. They squat where they are and kick a little dirt. The father is vaguely aware that there is a culture of hookworm in the mud along the river bank. He knows the children will get it on their bare feet.

But he hasn't the will nor the energy to resist. Too many things have happened to him. This is the lower class of the camp.

This is what the man in the tent will be in six months; what the man in the paper house with its peaked roof will be in a year, after his house has washed down and his children have sickened or died, after the loss of dignity and spirit have cut him down to a kind of sub-humanity.

Helpful strangers are not well received in this camp. The local sheriff makes a raid now and then for a wanted man, and if there is labor trouble the vigilantes may burn the poor houses. Social workers have taken case histories. They are filed and open for inspection. These families have been questioned over and over about their origins, number of children living and dead.

The information is taken down and filed. That is that. It has been done so often, and so little has come of it.

And there is another way for them to get attention. Let an epidemic break out, say typhoid or scarlet fever, and the county doctor will come to the camp and hurry the infected cases to the pesthouse. But malnutrition is not infectious, nor is dysentery, which is almost the rule among the children.

The county hospital has no room for measles, mumps, whooping cough; and yet these are often deadly to hunger-weakened children. And although we hear much about the free clinics for the poor, these people do not know how to get the aid and they do not get it. Also, since most of their dealings with authority are painful to them, they prefer not to take the chance.

This is the squatters' camp. Some are a little better, some much worse. I have described three typical families. In some of the camps there are as many as three hundred families like these. Some are so far from water that it must be bought at five cents a bucket.

And if these men steal, if there is developing among them a suspicion and hatred of well-dressed, satisfied people, the reason is not to be sought in their origin nor in any tendency to weakness in their character.

3. CORPORATION FARMING

When in the course of the season the small farmer has need of an influx of migrant workers he usually draws from the squatters' camps. By small farmer I mean the owner of the five- to hundred-acre farm, who operates and oversees his own farm.

Farms of this size are the greatest users of labor from the notorious squatters' camps. A few of the small farms set aside little pieces of land where the workers may pitch their shelters. Water is furnished, and once in a while a toilet. Rarely is there any facility for bathing. A small farm cannot afford the outlay necessary to maintain a sanitary camp.

Furthermore, the small farmers are afraid to allow groups of migrants to camp on their land, and they do not like the litter that is left when the men move on. On the whole, the relations between the migrants and the small farmer are friendly and understanding.

In many of California's agricultural strikes the small farmer has sided with the migrant against the powerful speculative farm groups. The workers realize that the problem of the small farmer is not unlike their own. We have the example in the San Joaquin Valley two years ago of a small farmer who sided with the workers in the cotton strike.

The speculative farm group, which is closely tied up with the power companies, determined to force this farm from opposition by cutting off the power necessary for irrigation.

But the strikers surrounded and held the power pole and refused to allow the current to be cut off. Incidents of this nature occur very frequently.

The small farmer, then, draws his labor from the squatters' camps and from the state and federal camps, which will be dealt with later.

On the other hand the large farms very often maintain their [own] camps for the laborers.

The large farms in California are organized as closely and are as centrally directed in their labor policy as are the industries and shipping, the banking and public utilities.

Indeed, such organizations as Associated Farmers, Inc. have as members and board members officials of banks, publishers of newspapers, and politicians; and through close association with the state Chamber of Commerce they have interlocking associations with shipowners' associations, public utilities corporations, and transportation companies.

Members of these speculative farm organizations are of several kinds—individual absentee owners of great tracts of land, banks that have acquired lands by foreclosure—for example, the tremendous Bank of America holdings in the San Joaquin Valley—and incorporated farms having stockholders, boards of directors, and the usual corporation approach.

These farms are invariably run by superintendents whose policies with regard to labor are directed from above. But the power of these organizations extends far beyond the governing of their own lands.

It is rare in California for a small farmer to be able to plant and mature his crops without loans from banks and finance companies. And since these banks and finance companies are at once members of the powerful growers' associations, and at the same time the one source of crop loans, the force of their policies on the small farmer can readily be seen. To refuse to obey is to invite foreclosure or a future denial of the necessary crop loan.

These strong groups, then, do not necessarily represent the general feeling toward labor; but being able to procure space in newspapers and on the radio, they are able not only to represent themselves as the whole body of California farmers, but are actually able to impose their policies on a great number of small farms.

The ranches operated by these speculative farmers usually have houses for the migrant laborers, houses for which they charge a rent of from $3 to $15 a month.

On most of the places it is not allowed that a worker refuse to pay the rent. If he wants to work he must live in the house, and the rent is taken from his first pay.

Let us see what this housing is like, not the $15 houses which can be rented only by field bosses (called pushers), but the $3 to $5 houses forced on the laborers.

The houses, one-room shacks usually about 10 by 12 feet, have no rug, no water, no bed. In one corner there is a little iron wood stove. Water must be carried from a faucet at the end of the street.

Also at the head of the street there will be either a dug toilet or a toilet with a septic tank to serve 100 to 150 people. A fairly typical ranch in Kern County had one bathhouse with a single shower and no heated water for the use of the whole block of houses, which had a capacity of 400 people.

The arrival of the migrant on such a ranch is something like this—he is assigned a house for his family; he may have from three to six children, but they must all live in the one room. He finds the ranch heavily policed by deputized employees.

The will of the ranch owner, then, is law; for these deputies are always on hand, their guns conspicuous. A disagreement constitutes resisting an officer. A glance at the list of migrants shot during a single year in California for "resisting an officer" will give a fair idea of the casualness of these "officers" in shooting workers.

The new arrival at the ranch will probably be without funds. His resources have been exhausted in getting here. But on many of the great ranches he will find a store run by the management at which he can get credit.

Thus he must work a second day to pay for his first, and so on. He is continually in debt. He must work. There is only one piece of property which is worth attaching for the debt, and that is his car; and while single men are able to get from harvest to harvest on the railroads and by hitchhiking, the man with a family will starve if he loses his car. Under this threat he must go on working.

In the field he will be continually attended by the "pusher," the field boss, and in many cases a pacer. In picking, a pacer will be a tree ahead of him. If he does not keep up he is fired. And it is often the case that the pacer's row is done over and over again afterward.

On these large ranches there is no attempt made for the relaxation or entertainment of the workers. Indeed, any attempt to congregate is broken up by deputies, for it is feared that if they are allowed to congregate they will organize, and that is the one thing the large ranches will not permit at any cost.

The attitude of the employer on the large ranch is one of

hatred and suspicion; his method is the threat of the deputies' guns.

The workers are herded about like animals. Every possible method is used to make them feel inferior and insecure. At the slightest suspicion that the men are organizing they are run from the ranch at the points of guns.

The large ranch owners know that if organization is ever effected there will be the expense of toilets, showers, decent living conditions, and a raise in wages.

The attitude of the workers on the large ranch is much that of the employer—hatred and suspicion. The worker sees himself surrounded by force. He knows that he can be murdered without fear on the part of the employer, and he has little recourse to law.

He has taken refuge in a sullen, tense quiet. He cannot resist the credit that allows him to feed his family, but he knows perfectly well the reason for the credit.

There are a few large ranches in California which maintain "model houses" for the workers, neatly painted buildings with some conveniences.

These ranches usually charge a rent of $5 a month for a single-room house and pay 33⅓ per cent less than the prevailing wage.

The labor policy of these absentee-directed large farms has created the inevitable result. Usually there are guards at the gates, the roads are patrolled, permission to inspect the premises is never given.

It would almost seem that having built the repressive attitude toward the labor they need to survive, the directors were terrified of the things they have created.

This fear dictates an increase of the repressive method, a greater number of guards, and a constant suggestion that the ranch is armed to fight.

Here, as in the squatters' camps, the dignity of the men is attacked. No trust is accorded them. They are surrounded as though it were suspected that they would break into revolt at any moment. It would seem that a surer method of forcing them to revolt could not be devised.

This repressive method results inevitably in flares of disorganized revolt which must be put down by force and by increased intimidation.

The large growers' groups have found the law inadequate to their uses; and they have become so powerful that such charges as felonious assault, mayhem and inciting to riot, kidnaping and flogging cannot be brought against them in the controlled courts.

The attitude of the large growers' associations toward labor is best stated by Hugh T. Osburne, a member of the Board of Supervisors of Imperial County and active in the Imperial County Associated Farmers group. Before the judiciary committee of the California Assembly he said:

"In Imperial Valley we don't need this criminal syndicalism law. They have got to have it for the rest of the counties that don't know how to handle these matters. We don't need it because we have worked out our own way of handling these things. We won't have another of these trials. We have a better way of doing it. Trials cost too much."

"The better way," as accepted by the large growers of the Imperial Valley, includes a system of terrorism that would be unusual in the Fascist nations of the world. The stupid policy of the large grower and the absentee speculative farmer in California has accomplished nothing but unrest, tension, and hatred. A continuation of this approach constitutes a criminal endangering of the peace of the state.

4. GOVERNMENT HOUSING

The federal government, realizing that the miserable condition of the California migrant agricultural worker constitutes an immediate and vital problem, has set up two camps for the moving workers and contemplates eight more in the immediate future. The development of the camps at Arvin and Marysville makes a social and economic study of vast interest.

The present camps are set upon leased ground. Future camps are to be constructed on land purchased by the government. The government provides places for tents. Permanent structures are simple, including washrooms, toilets and showers, an administration building, and a place where the people can entertain themselves. The equipment at the Arvin camp, exclusive of rent of the land, cost approximately $18,000.

At this camp water, toilet paper and some medical supplies are provided. A resident manager is on the ground. Campers are received on the following conditions: (1) that the men are bona-fide farm people and intend to work, (2) that they will help to maintain the cleanliness of the camp, and (3) that in lieu of rent they will devote two hours a week toward the maintenance and improvement of the camp.

The result has been more than could be expected. From the first, the intent of the management has been to restore the dignity and decency that had been kicked out of the migrants by their intolerable mode of life.

In this pamphlet the word "dignity" has been used several times. It has been used not as some attitude of self-importance, but simply as a register of a man's responsibility to the community.

A man herded about, surrounded by armed guards, starved, and forced to live in filth loses his dignity; that is, he loses his valid position in regard to society, and consequently his whole ethics toward society. Nothing is a better example of this than the prison, where the men are reduced to no dignity and where crimes and infractions of rule are constant.

We regard this destruction of dignity, then, as one of the most regrettable results of the migrant's life, since it does reduce his responsibility and does make him a sullen outcast who will strike at our government in any way that occurs to him.

The example at Arvin adds weight to such a conviction. The

people in the camp are encouraged to govern themselves, and they have responded with simple and workable democracy. The camp is divided into four units. Each unit, by direct election, is represented in a central governing committee, an entertainment committee, a maintenance committee, and a Good Neighbors committee. Each of these members is elected by the vote of his unit, and is recallable by the same vote.

The manager, of course, has the right to veto, but he practically never finds it necessary to act contrary to the recommendations of the committee.

The result of this responsible self-government has been remarkable. The inhabitants of the camp came there beaten, sullen, and destitute. But as their social sense was revived they have settled down. The camp takes care of its own destitute, feeding and sheltering those who have nothing with their own poor stores. The central committee makes the laws that govern the conduct of the inhabitants.

In the year that the Arvin camp has been in operation there has not been any need for outside police. Punishments are the restrictions of certain privileges such as admission to the community dances, or for continued anti-social conduct a recommendation to the manager that the culprit be ejected from the camp.

A works committee assigns the labor to be done in the camp, improvements, garbage disposal, maintenance, and repairs. The entertainment committee arranges for the weekly dances, the music for which is furnished by an orchestra made up of the inhabitants.

So well do they play that one orchestra has been lost to the radio already. The committee also takes care of the many self-made games and courts that have been built.

The Good Neighbors, a women's organization, takes part in quilting and sewing projects, sees that destitution does not exist, governs and watches the nursery, where children can be left while the mothers are working in the fields and in the packing sheds. And all this is done with the outside aid of one manager and one part-time nurse. As experiments in natural and democratic self-government, these camps are unique in the United States.

In visiting these camps one is impressed with several things in particular. The sullenness and frightened expression that is the rule among the migrants has disappeared from the faces of the federal-camp inhabitants. Instead there is a steadiness of gaze and a self-confidence that can only come of restored dignity.

The difference seems to lie in the new position of the migrant in the community. Before he came to the camp he had been policed, hated, and moved about. It had been made clear that he was not wanted.

In the federal camps every effort of the management is expended to give him his place in society. There are no persons on relief in these camps.

In the Arvin camp the central committee recommended the expulsion of a family which applied for relief. Employment is more common than in any similar group for, having something of their own, these men are better workers. The farmers in the vicinity seem to prefer the camp men to others.

The inhabitants of the federal camps are no picked group. They are typical of the new migrants. They come from Oklahoma, Arkansas, and Texas and the other drought states. Eighty-five per cent of them are former farm owners, farm renters, or farm laborers. The remaining fifteen per cent includes painters, mechanics, electricians and even professional men.

When a new family enters one of these camps it is usually dirty, tired, and broken. A group from the Good Neighbors meets it, tells it the rules, helps it to get settled, instructs it in the use of the sanitary facilities, and, if there are insufficient blankets or shelters, furnishes them from its own stores.

The children are bathed and cleanly dressed and the needs of the future canvassed. If the children have not enough clothes the community sewing circle will get busy immediately. In case any of the family are sick the camp manager or the part-time nurse is called and treatment is carried out.

These Good Neighbors are not trained social workers, but they have what is perhaps more important, an understanding which grows from a likeness of experience. Nothing has happened to the newcomer that has not happened to the committee.

A typical manager's report is as follows:

"New arrivals. Low on foodstuffs. Most of the personal belongings were tied up in sacks and were in a filthy condition. The Good Neighbors at once took the family in hand, and by ten o'clock they were fed, washed, camped, settled, and asleep."

These two camps each accommodate about 200 families. They were started as experiments, and the experiments have proven successful. Between the rows of tents the families have started little gardens for the raising of vegetables, and the plots, which must be cared for after a ten- or twelve-hour day of work, produce beets, cabbages, corn, carrots, onions, and turnips. The passion to produce is very great. One man, who has not yet been assigned to his little garden plot, is hopefully watering a Jimson weed simply to have something of his own growing.

The federal government, through the Resettlement Administration, plans to extend these camps and to include with them small maintenance farms. These are intended to solve several problems.

They will allow the women and children to stay in one place, permitting the children to go to school and the women to maintain the farms during the work times of the men. They will reduce the degenerating effect of the migrants' life, they will re-instill the sense of government and possession that has been lost by the migrants.

Located near the areas which demand seasonal labor, these communities will permit these subsistence farmers to work in the harvests, while at the same time they stop the wanderings over the whole state. The success of these federal camps in making potential criminals into citizens makes the usual practice of expending money on tear gas seem a little silly.

The greater part of the new migrants from the dust bowl will become permanent California citizens. They have shown in these camps an ability to produce and to cooperate. They are passionately determined to make their living on the land. One of them said, "If it's work you got to do mister, we'll do it. Our folks never did take charity and this family ain't takin' it now."

The plan of the Resettlement Administration to extend these federal camps is being fought by certain interests in California. The arguments against the camps are as follows:

That they will increase the need for locally paid police. But the two camps already carried on for over a year have proved to need no locally paid police whatever, while the squatters' camps are a constant charge on the sheriffs' offices.

The second argument is that the cost of schools to the district will be increased. School allotments are from the state and governed by the number of pupils. And even if it did cost more, the communities need the work of these families and must assume some responsibility for them. The alternative is a generation of illiterates.

The third is that they will lower the land values because of the type of people inhabiting the camps. Those camps already established have in no way affected the value of the land and the people are of good American stock who have proved that they can maintain an American standard of living. The cleanliness and lack of disease in the two experimental camps are proof of this.

The fourth argument, as made by the editor of *The Yuba City Herald,* a self-admitted sadist who wrote a series of incendiary and subversive editorials concerning the Marysville camp, is that these are the breeding places for strikes.

Under pressure of evidence the Yuba City patriot withdrew his contention that the camp was full of radicals. This will be the argument used by the speculative growers' associations.

These associations have said in so many words that they require a peon class to succeed. Any action to better the condition of the migrant will be considered radical to them.

5. RELIEF, MEDICINE, INCOME, DIET

Migrant families in California find that unemployment relief, which is available to settled unemployed, has little to offer them. In the first place, there has grown up a regular technique for getting relief; one who knows the ropes can find aid from the various state and federal disbursement agencies, while a man ignorant of the methods will be turned away.

The migrant is always partially unemployed. The nature of his occupation makes his work seasonal. At the same time the nature of his work makes him ineligible for relief. The basis for receiving most of the relief is residence.

But it is impossible for the migrant to accomplish the residence. He must move about the country. He could not stop long enough to establish residence or he would starve to death. He finds, then, on application, that he cannot be put on the relief rolls. And being ignorant, he gives up at that point.

For the same reason he finds that he cannot receive any of the local benefits reserved for residents of a county. The county hospital was built not for the transient, but for residents of the county.

It will be interesting to trace the history of one family in relation to medicine, work relief, and direct relief. The family consisted of five persons, a man of fifty, his wife of forty-five, two boys, fifteen and twelve, and a girl of six. They came from Oklahoma, where the father operated a little ranch of fifty acres of prairie.

When the ranch dried up and blew away the family put its movable possessions in an old Dodge truck and came to California. They arrived in time for the orange picking in southern California and put in a good average season.

The older boy and the father together made $60. At that

time the automobile broke out some teeth of the differential and the repairs, together with three second-hand tires, took $22. The family moved into Kern County to chop grapes and camped in the squatters' camp on the edge of Bakersfield.

At this time the father sprained his ankle and the little girl developed measles. Doctors' bills amounted to $10 of the remaining store, and food and transportation took most of the rest.

The fifteen-year-old boy was now the only earner in the family. The twelve-year-old boy picked up a brass gear in a yard and took it to sell.

He was arrested and taken before the juvenile court, but was released to his father's custody. The father walked in to Bakersfield from the squatters' camp on a sprained ankle because the gasoline was gone from the automobile and he didn't dare invest any of the remaining money in more gasoline.

This walk caused complications in the sprain which laid him up again. The little girl had recovered from measles by this time, but her eyes had not been protected and she had lost part of her eyesight.

The father now applied for relief and found that he was ineligible because he had not established the necessary residence. All resources were gone. A little food was given to the family by neighbors in the squatters' camp.

A neighbor who had a goat brought in a cup of milk every day for the little girl.

At this time the fifteen-year-old boy came home from the fields with a pain in his side. He was feverish and in great pain.

The mother put hot cloths on his stomach while a neighbor took the crippled father to the county hospital to apply for aid. The hospital was full, all its time taken by bona-fide local residents. The trouble described as a pain in the stomach by the father was not taken seriously.

The father was given a big dose of salts to take home to the boy. That night the pain grew so great that the boy became unconscious. The father telephoned the hospital and found that there was no one on duty who could attend to his case. The boy died of a burst appendix the next day.

There was no money. The county buried him free. The father sold the Dodge for $30 and bought a $2 wreath for the funeral. With the remaining money he laid in a store of cheap, filling food—beans, oatmeal, lard. He tried to go back to work in the fields. Some of the neighbors gave him rides to work and charged him a small amount for transportation.

He was on the weak ankle too soon and could not make over seventy-five cents a day at piece-work chopping. Again he applied for relief and was refused because he was not a resident and because he was employed. The little girl, because of insufficient food and weakness from measles, relapsed into influenza.

The father did not try the county hospital again. He went to a private doctor who refused to come to the squatters' camp unless he were paid in advance. The father took two days' pay and gave it to the doctor, who came to the family shelter, took the girl's temperature, gave the mother seven pills, told the mother to keep the child warm, and went away. The father lost his job because he was too slow.

He applied again for help and was given one week's supply of groceries.

This can go on indefinitely. The case histories like it can be found in their thousands. It may be argued that there were ways for this man to get aid, but how did he know where to get it? There was no way for him to find out.

California communities have used the old, old methods of dealing with such problems. The first method is to disbelieve it and vigorously to deny that there is a problem. The second is to deny local responsibility since the people are not permanent residents. And the third and silliest of all is to run the trouble over the county borders into another county. The floater method of swapping what the counties consider undesirables from hand to hand is like a game of medicine ball.

A fine example of this insular stupidity concerns the hookworm situation in Stanislaus County. The mud along water courses where there are squatters living is infected. Several businessmen of Modesto and Ceres offered as a solution that the squatters be cleared out. There was no thought of isolating the victims and stopping the hookworm.

The affected people were, according to these men, to be run out of the county to spread the disease in other fields. It is this refusal of the counties to consider anything but the immediate economy and profit of the locality that is the cause of a great deal of the unsolvable quality of the migrants' problem. The counties seem terrified that they may be required to give some aid to the labor they require for their harvests.

According to several government and state surveys and studies of large numbers of migrants, the maximum a worker can make is $400 a year, while the average is around $300, and the large minimum is $150 a year. This amount must feed, clothe, and transport whole families.

Sometimes whole families are able to work in the fields, thus making an additional wage. In other observed cases a whole family, weakened by sickness and malnutrition, has worked in the fields, making less than the wage of one healthy man. It does not take long at the migrants' work to reduce the health of any family. Food is scarce always, and luxuries of any kind are unknown.

Observed diets run something like this when the family is making money:

Family of eight—Boiled cabbage, baked sweet potatoes, creamed carrots, beans, fried dough, jelly, tea.

Family of seven—Beans, baking-powder biscuits, jam, coffee.

Family of six—Canned salmon, cornbread, raw onions.

Family of five—Biscuits, fried potatoes, dandelion greens, pears.

These are dinners—it is to be noticed that even in these flush times there is no milk, no butter. The major part of the diet is starch. In slack times the diet becomes all starch, this being the cheapest way to fill up. Dinners during layoffs are as follows:

Family of eight (there were six children)—Dandelion greens and boiled potatoes.

Family of seven—Beans, fried dough.

Family of six—Fried cornmeal.

Family of five—Oatmeal mush.

It will be seen that even in flush times the possibility of remaining healthy is very slight. The complete absence of milk for the children is responsible for many of the diseases of malnutrition. Even pellagra is far from unknown.

The preparation of food is the most primitive. Cooking equipment usually consists of a hole dug in the ground or a kerosene can with a smoke vent and an open front.

If the adults have been working ten hours in the fields or in the packing sheds they do not want to cook. They will buy canned goods as long as they have money, and when they are low in funds they will subsist on half-cooked starches.

The problem of childbirth among the migrants is among the most terrible. There is no prenatal care of the mothers whatever, and no possibility of such care. They must work in the fields until they are physically unable or, if they do not work, the care of the other children and of the camp will not allow the prospective mothers any rest.

In actual birth the presence of a doctor is a rare exception. Sometimes in the squatters' camps a neighbor woman will help at the birth. There will be no sanitary precautions nor hygienic arrangements. The child will be born on newspapers in the dirty bed. In case of a bad presentation requiring surgery or forceps, the mother is practically condemned to death. Once born, the eyes of the baby are not treated; the endless medical attention lavished on middle-class babies is completely absent.

The mother, usually suffering from malnutrition, is not able to produce breast milk. Sometimes the baby is nourished on canned milk until it can eat fried dough and cornmeal. This being the case, the infant mortality is very great.

The following is an example: Wife of family with three children. She is thirty-eight; her face is lined and thin and there is a hard glaze on her eyes. The three children who survive were born prior to 1929, when the family rented a farm in Utah. In 1930 this woman bore a child which lived four months and died of "colic."

In 1931 her child was born dead because "a han' truck fulla boxes run inta me two days before the baby come." In 1932 there was a miscarriage. "I couldn't carry the baby 'cause I was sick." She is ashamed of this. In 1933 her baby lived a week. "Jus' died. I don't know what of." In 1934 she had no pregnancy. She is also a little ashamed of this. In 1935 her baby lived a long time, nine months.

"Seemed for a long time like he was gonna live. Big strong fella it seemed like." She is pregnant again now. "If we could get milk for um I guess it'd be better." This is an extreme case, but by no means an unusual one.

6. The Foreign Migrant

The history of California's importation and treatment of foreign labor is a disgraceful picture of greed and cruelty. The first importations of large groups consisted of thousands of Chinese, brought in as cheap labor to build the transcontinental railroads. When the roads were completed a few of the Chinese were retained as section hands, but the bulk went as cheap farm labor.

The traditional standard of living of the Chinese was so low that white labor could not compete with it. At the same time the family organizations allowed them to procure land and to make it produce far more than could the white men. Consequently white labor began a savage warfare on the coolies.

Feeling against them ran high and culminated in riots which gradually drove the Chinese from the fields, while immigration laws closed the borders to new influxes.

The Japanese were the next people encouraged to come in as cheap labor, and the history of their activities was almost exactly like that of the Chinese: a low standard of living which allowed them to accumulate property while at the same time they took the jobs of white labor.

And again there were riots and land laws and closed borders. The feeling against the Japanese culminated in the whole "yellow peril" literature which reached its peak just before the war.

The Japanese as a threat to white labor were removed. Some of them had acquired land, some went to the cities, and large numbers of them were moved or deported. The Japanese farm laborers, although unorganized, developed a kind of spontaneous organization which made them less tractable than the Chinese had been.

But, as usual, the nature of California's agriculture made the owners of farm land cry for peon labor. In the early part of the century another source of cheap labor became available.

Mexicans were imported in large numbers, and the standard of living they were capable of maintaining depressed the wages of farm labor to a point where the white could not compete. By 1920 there were 80,000 foreign-born Mexicans in California. The opening of the intensive farming in the Imperial Valley and southern California made necessary the use of this cheap labor.

And at about this time the demand for peon labor began to come more and more from the large growers and the developing shipper-growers. When the imposition of a quota was suggested the small farmers (five to twenty acres) had no objection to the restriction, and 66 per cent were actively in favor of the quota.

The large grower, on the other hand, was opposed to the quota. Seventy-eight per cent were openly opposed to any restriction on the importation of peon labor. With the depression, farm wages sunk to such a low in the southern part of the state that white labor could not exist on them. Fourteen cents an hour became the standard wage.

To the large grower the Mexican labor offered more advantages than simply its cheapness. It could be treated as so much scrap when it was not needed. Any local care for the sick and crippled could be withheld; and in addition, if it offered any resistance to the low wage or the terrible living conditions, it could be deported to Mexico at government expense.

Recently, led by the example of the workers in Mexico, the Mexicans in California have begun to organize. Their organization in southern California has been met with vigilante terrorism and savagery unbelievable in a civilized state.

Concerning these repressive activities of the large growers, a special commission's report to the National Labor Relations Board has this to say: "Fundamentally, much of the trouble with Mexican labor in the Imperial Valley lies in the natural desire of the workers to organize.

"Their efforts have been thwarted or rendered ineffective by a well-organized opposition against them. We uncovered sufficient evidence to convince us that in more than one instance the law was trampled under foot by representative citizens of Imperial Valley and by public officials under oath to support the law."

The report lists a number of such outrages. "Large numbers of men and women arrested but not booked . . . intimidation used to force pleas of guilty to felonious charges . . . bail was set so large that release was impossible." This report further says: "In our opinion, regular peace officers and civilians displayed pistols too freely, and the police unwarrantly [sic] used tear-gas bombs.

"We do not understand why approximately eighty officers

found it necessary to gas an audience of several hundred men and women and children in a comparatively small one-story building while searching for three 'agitators.' "

The right of free speech, the right of assembly, and the right of jury trial are not extended to Mexicans in the Imperial Valley.

This treatment of Mexican labor, together with the deportation of large groups and the plan of the present Mexican government for repatriating its nationals, is gradually withdrawing Mexican labor from the fields of California. As with the Chinese and Japanese, they have committed the one crime that will not be permitted by the large growers.

They have attempted to organize for their own protection. It is probable that Mexican labor will not long be available to California agriculture.

The last great source of foreign labor to be furnished the California grower has been the Filipino. Between 1920 and 1929 31,000 of these little brown men were brought to the United States, and most of them remained in California, a new group of peon workers.

They were predominantly young, male and single. Their women were not brought with them. The greatest number of them found agricultural employment in central and northern California. Their wages are the lowest paid to any migratory labor.

As in the case of the Mexicans, Japanese, and Chinese, the Filipinos have been subjected to racial discrimination.

They are unique in California agriculture. Being young, male, and single, they form themselves into natural groups of five, six, eight; they combine their resources in the purchase of equipment, such as autos. Their group life constitutes a lesson in economy.

A labor coordinator of the State Relief Administration has said, "They often subsist for a week on a double handful of rice and a little bread."

These young men were not permitted to bring their women.

At the same time the marriage laws of California were amended to include persons of the Malay race among those peoples who cannot intermarry with whites. Since they were young and male, the one outlet for their amorous energies lay in extra-legal arrangements with white women.

This not only gained for them a reputation for immorality, but was the direct cause of many race riots directed against them.

They were good workers, but like the earlier immigrants they committed the unforgivable in trying to organize for their own protection. Their organization brought on them the usual terrorism.

A fine example of this was the vigilante raid in the Salinas valley last year when a bunkhouse was burned down and all the possessions of the Filipinos destroyed.

In this case the owner of the bunkhouse collected indemnity for the loss of his property. Although the Filipinos have brought suit, no settlement has as yet been made for them.

But the Filipino is not long to be a factor in California agriculture. With the establishment of the Philippine Islands as an autonomous nation, the 35,000 Filipinos in California have suddenly become aliens.

The federal government, in cooperation with the Philippine government, has started a campaign to repatriate all of the Filipinos in California. It is only a question of time before this is accomplished.

The receding waves of foreign peon labor are leaving California agriculture to the mercies of our own people. The old methods of intimidation and starvation perfected against the foreign peons are being used against the new white migrant workers. But they will not be successful.

Consequently, California agriculture must begin some kind of stock-taking, some reorganization of its internal economy. Farm labor in California will be white labor, it will be American labor, and it will insist on a standard of living much higher than that which was accorded the foreign "cheap labor."

Some of the more enlightened of the large growers argue for white labor on the ground "that it will not go on relief as quickly as the Mexican labor has."

These enthusiasts do not realize that the same pride and self-respect that deters white migrant labor from accepting charity and relief, if there is an alternative, will also cause the white American labor to refuse to accept the role of field peon, with its attendant terrorism, squalor, and starvation.

Foreign labor is on the wane in California, and the future farm workers are to be white and American. This fact must be recognized and a rearrangement of the attitude toward and treatment of migrant labor must be achieved.

7. THE FUTURE?

From almost daily news stories, from a great number of government reports available to anyone who is interested, and from this necessarily short pamphlet, it becomes apparent that some plan must be contrived to take care of the problem of the migrants. If for no humanitarian reason, the need of California agriculture for these people dictates the necessity of such a plan. A survey of the situation makes a few suggestions obvious:

There should be established in the state a migratory labor board with branches in the various parts of the state which require seasonal labor. On this board labor should be represented.

Local committees should, before the seasonal demand for labor, canvass the district, discover and publish the amount of labor needed and the wages to be paid.

Such information should then be placed in the hands of the labor unions, so that the harvest does not become a great, disorganized gold rush with twice and three times as much labor applying as is needed.

It has long been the custom of the shipper-grower, the speculative farmer, and the corporation farm to encourage twice as much labor to come to a community as could be possibly used. With an over-supply of labor, wages could be depressed below any decent standard. Such a suggested labor board (if it had a strong labor representation) would put a stop to such tactics.

Agricultural workers should be encouraged and helped to organize, both for their own protection, for the intelligent distribution of labor, and for their self-government through the consideration of their own problems.

The same arguments are used against the organizing of agricultural labor as were used sixty years ago against the organizing of the craft and skilled labor unions. It was urged then that industry could not survive if labor were organized. It is argued today that agriculture cannot exist if farm labor is organized. It is reasonable to believe that agriculture would suffer no more from organization than industry has.

It is certain that until agricultural labor is organized, and until the farm laborer is represented in the centers where his wage is decided, wages will continue to be depressed and living conditions will grow increasingly impossible until from pain, hunger, and despair the whole mass of labor will revolt.

The attorney general, who has been given power in such matters, should investigate and trace to its source any outbreak of the vigilante terrorism which is the disgrace of California. Inspiration for such outbreaks is limited to a few individuals.

It should be as easy for an unbought investigation to hunt them down as it was for the government to hunt down kidnapers. Since a government is its system of laws and since armed vigilantism is an attempt to overthrow that system of laws and to substitute a government by violence, prosecution could be carried out on the grounds of guilt under the criminal syndicalism laws already on our statute books.

These laws have been used only against workers. Let them be equally used on the more deadly fascistic groups which preach and act the overthrow of our form of government by force of arms.

If these suggestions could be carried out, a good part of the disgraceful condition of agricultural labor in California might be alleviated.

If, on the other hand, as has been stated by a large grower, our agriculture requires the creation and maintenance at any cost of a peon class, then it is submitted that California agriculture is economically unsound under a democracy.

And if the terrorism and reduction of human rights, the floggings, murder by deputies, kidnapings, and refusal of trial by jury are necessary to our economic security, it is further submitted that California democracy is rapidly dwindling away. Fascistic methods are more numerous, more powerfully applied, and more openly practiced in California than any other place in the United States.

It will require a militant and watchful organization of middle-class people, workers, teachers, craftsmen, and liberals to fight this encroaching social philosophy, and to maintain this state in a democratic form of government.

The new migrants to California from the dust bowl are here to stay. They are of the best American stock, intelligent, resourceful, and, if given a chance, socially responsible.

To attempt to force them into a peonage of starvation and intimidated despair will be unsuccessful. They can be citizens of the highest type, or they can be an army driven by suffering and hatred to take what they need. On their future treatment will depend which course they will be forced to take.

EPILOGUE: SPRING 1938*

The spring is rich and green in California this year. In the fields the wild grass is ten inches high, and in the orchards and vineyards the grass is deep and nearly ready to be plowed under to enrich the soil. Already the flowers are starting to bloom.

* Compare this added passage especially with Chapter Twenty-five of the novel.—ED.

Very shortly one of the oil companies will be broadcasting the locations of the wild-flower masses. It is a beautiful spring.

There has been no war in California, no plague, no bombing of open towns and roads, no shelling of cities. It is a beautiful year. And thousands of families are starving in California. In the county seats the coroners are filling in "malnutrition" in the spaces left for "causes of death." For some reason, a coroner shrinks from writing "starvation" when a thin child is dead in a tent.

For it's in the tents you see along the roads and in the shacks built from dump heap materials that the hunger is, and it isn't malnutrition. It is starvation. Malnutrition means you go without certain food essentials and take a long time to die, but starvation means no food at all. The green grass is spreading right into the tent doorways and the orange trees are loaded. In the cotton fields, a few wisps of the old crop cling to the black stems. But the people who picked the cotton, and cut the peaches and apricots, who crawled all day in the rows of lettuce and beans are hungry. The men who harvested the crops of California, the women and girls who stood all day and half the night in the canneries, are starving.

It was so two years ago in Nipomo, it is so now, it will continue to be so until the rich produce of California can be grown and harvested on some other basis than that of stupidity and greed.

What is to be done about it? The federal government is trying to feed and give direct relief, but it is difficult to do quickly for there are forms to fill out, questions to ask, for fear someone who isn't actually starving may get something. The state relief organizations are trying to send those who haven't been in the state for a year back to the states they came from. The Associated Farmers, which presumes to speak for the farms of California and which is made up of such earth-stained toilers as chain banks, public utilities, railroad companies, and those huge corporations called land companies—this financial organization in the face of the crisis is conducting Americanism meetings and bawling about Reds and foreign agitators. It has been invariably true in the past that when such a close-knit financial group as the Associated Farmers becomes excited about our ancient liberties and foreign agitators, someone is about to lose something. A wage cut has invariably followed such a campaign of pure Americanism. And of course any resentment of such a wage cut is set down as the work of foreign agitators. Anyway, that is the Associated Farmers' contribution to the hunger of the men and women who harvest their crops. The small farmers, who do not belong to the Associated Farmers and cannot make use of the slop chest, are helpless to do anything about it. The little storekeepers at crossroads and in small towns have carried the accounts of the working people until they are near to bankruptcy.

And there are 1000 families in Tulare County, and 2000 families in Kings County, 1500 families in Kern County, and so on. The families average three persons, by the way. With the exception of a little pea picking, there isn't going to be any work for nearly three months.

There is sickness in the tents, pneumonia and measles, tuberculosis. Measles in a tent, with no way to protect the eyes, means a child with weakened eyes for life. And there are the various diseases attributable to hunger—rickets, and the beginning of pellagra. The nurses in the counties, and there aren't one-tenth enough of them, are working their heads off, doing a magnificent job, and they can only begin to do the work. The corps includes nurses assigned by the federal and state public-health services, school nurses and county health nurses and a few nurses furnished by the Council of Women for Home Missions, a national church organization. I've seen them, red-eyed, weary from far too many hours, and seeming to make no impression in the illness about them.

It may be of interest to reiterate the reasons why these people are in the state and the reason they must go hungry. They are here because we need them. Before the white American migrants were here, it was the custom in California to import great numbers of Mexicans, Filipinos, Japanese, to keep them segregated, to herd them about like animals, and, if there were any complaints, to deport or to imprison the leaders. This system of labor was a dream of heaven to such employers as those who now fear foreign agitators so much.

But then the dust and the tractors began displacing the sharecroppers of Oklahoma, Texas, Kansas, and Arkansas. Families who had lived for many years on the little "croppers lands" were dispossessed because the land was in the hands of the banks and the finance companies and because these owners found that one man with a tractor could do the work of ten sharecropper families. Faced with the question of starving or moving, these dispossessed families came west. To a certain extent they were actuated by advertisements and handbills distributed by labor contractors from California. It is to the advantage of the corporate farmer to have too much labor, for then wages can be cut. Then people who are hungry will fight each other for a job rather than the employer for a living wage.

It is possible to make money for food and gasoline for at least nine months of the year if you are quick on the getaway, if your wife and your children work in the fields. But then the dead three months strikes, and what can you do then? The migrant cannot save anything. It takes everything he can make to feed his family and buy gasoline to go to the next job. If you don't believe this, go out in the cotton fields next year. Work all day and see if you have made thirty-five cents. A good picker makes more, of course, but you can't.

The method for concentrating labor for one of the great crops is this. Handbills are distributed, advertisements are printed. You've seen them. Cotton pickers wanted in Bakersfield or Fresno or Imperial Valley. Then all the available migrants rush to the scene. They arrive with no money and little food. The reserve has been spent getting there. If wages happen to drop a little, they must take them anyway. The moment the crop is picked, the locals begin to try to get rid of the people who have harvested their crops. They want to run them out, move them on. The county hospitals are closed to them. They are not eligible [for] relief. You must be eligible to eat. That particular locality is through with them until another crop comes in.

It will be remembered that two years ago some so-called agitators were tarred and feathered. The population of migrants left the locality just as the hops were ripe. Then the howling of the locals was terrible to hear. They even tried to get the Army and the C.C.C. ordered to pick their crops.

About the fifteenth of January the dead time sets in. There is no work. First the gasoline gives out. And without gasoline a man cannot go to a job even if he could get one. Then the food goes. And then in the rains, with insufficient food, the children develop colds because the ground in the tents is wet. I talked to a man last week who lost two children in ten days with pneumonia. His face was hard and fierce and he didn't talk much. I talked to a girl with a baby and offered her a cigarette. She took two puffs and vomited in the street. She was ashamed. She shouldn't have tried to smoke, she said, for she hadn't eaten for two days. I heard a [woman] whimpering that the baby was sucking but nothing came out of the breast. I heard a man explain very shyly that his little girl couldn't go to school because she was too weak to walk to school and besides the school lunches of the other children made her unhappy. I heard a man tell in a monotone how he couldn't get a doctor while his oldest boy died of pneumonia but that a doctor came right away after [he] was dead. It is easy to get a doctor to look at a corpse, not so easy to get one for a live person. It is easy to get a body buried. A truck comes right out and takes it away. The state is much more interested in how you die than in how you live. The man who was telling about it had just found that out. He didn't want to believe it.

Next year the hunger will come again, and the year after that, and so on, until we come out of this coma and realize that our agriculture for all its great produce is a failure. If you buy a farm horse and feed him only when you work him, the horse will die. No one complains at the necessity of feeding the horse when he is not working. But we complain about feeding the men and women who work our lands. Is it possible that this state is so stupid, so vicious and so greedy that it cannot feed and clothe the men and women who help to make it the richest area in the world? Must the hunger become anger and the anger fury before anything will be done?

CHAPTER 4

What Became of the Joads?

The Grapes of Wrath ENDS WITH THOSE MEMBERS OF THE Joad family who have stayed together gathered in a barn during a torrential rain, their problems of finding work and a home still unsolved. Readers who crave more definite conclusions are likely to ask, "What became of the Joads?" Actually they are asking two closely related questions: What happened to the family in the novel? and What happened to the whole group of migrants that this family represents?

Since *The Grapes of Wrath* is a novel and not a tract, the ending is intentionally inconclusive. Steinbeck is not telling readers what became of the Joads; rather, he is asking what is going to become of them. Like Prospero in the Epilogue to Shakespeare's *Tempest*, he leaves the disposition of the characters to the "indulgence" of the reader.

The story that Steinbeck sought to tell does end, furthermore, with Ma Joad's discovery that it is no longer the "fambly" alone that one must "give a han'," but "everybody." As I wrote in my own study of Steinbeck,* answering the charge that the tale is inconclusive, the scene in the barn "marks the end of the story that Steinbeck has

* *John Steinbeck* by Warren French (New York: Twayne, 1961), p. 107.

to tell about the Joads," because "their education is completed. . . . What happens to them now depends upon the ability of the rest of society to learn the same lesson they have already learned."

The question of what actually became of the horde of migrants is more difficult to answer. Apparently no one has ever tried to trace the whereabouts of the individuals who once lived in the roadside camps and sought work in overcrowded fields. Americans seldom concern themselves with such questions. The stock in trade of our newspapers is the scare headline and the sensational exposé; once the sensation is past, the subject is no longer newsworthy. Even a diligent sociologist who might want to pursue the question would be deterred by the reluctance of ex-"Okies" to identify themselves. Much as Americans are inclined to boast of their humble origins, they wish to forget "shameful" episodes of the past.

To answer the question generally: in one important sense the migrants have not disappeared. As David Burgess, almost alone among reporters, kept reminding readers of *The New Republic* during World War II, migrant laborers were still living under subhuman conditions even at the height of the wartime labor boom. "Harvest of Shame," Edward R. Murrow's controversial CBS television documentary on the plight of transient field workers in Florida, reminded us in November 1960 that the migrants remain with us. Ernesto Galarza, secretary-treasurer of the National Agricultural Workers Union (AFL-CIO), in his pamphlet "Strangers in Our Fields" and other reports, maintains that the same California groups that exploited the Okies are attempting even today to lower wages, profit from workers' ignorance, and control the labor supply in such a way as to crowd out experienced domestic workers acquainted with their rights.

Yet it is misleading to call the migrants of the forties and later "Joads," after Steinbeck's characters. As Carey Mc-Williams has pointed out, workers all over the country were following seasonal crops long before the thirties, and probably such workers will always be needed in some areas. They are an essential if much-abused part of American agriculture. Steinbeck's Joads, however, belong in a special category; they were not habitual migrants, nor did they wish to remain migratory. They were not, like many migratory workers, members of minority racial or national groups. They were descendants of the pioneering American farmers who had tamed the Midwestern prairies. They had been forced by the drought from lands that they had abused; and, in the manner of their forefathers, they sought new permanent farmsteads in more promising regions. Steinbeck made no pretense, either in *Their Blood Is Strong* or in *The Grapes of Wrath*, of dealing dispassionately with the whole vast problem of migratory labor in the United States. He sought to warn against the conversion of proud and independent-minded American citizens into a permanent peon class.

Migrants like the Joads created an unprecedented emergency because, before those who sought to manipulate the supply of agricultural workers in order to depress wages and increase profits realized what was happening, the dispossessed Midwesterners had temporarily swelled the ranks of the migratory laborers beyond the ability of Pacific Coast farms to absorb them. The migrants were in actuality surplus population, and—as Carey McWilliams says—they were shuffled about irresponsibly by frantic state and local authorities in the hope that they might simply disappear. The earlier and later migrants were generally easily oppressed people, ignorant of their rights and easily awed by power; though they were and are blots on America's social landscape, they have created no such critical emergencies as the "Joads" did in their struggle for sheer survival. The stubborn refusal of the Midwestern outcasts to "disappear" posed a problem that Californians approached not calmly and judiciously but hysterically, out of the mixture of fear and intellectual inertia that often characterizes "respectable" Americans.

Three things can be said at once of the victims of this hysteria. First, few of them went home. A conspicuous feature of the rural landscape of Oklahoma, Kansas, Texas, and Missouri even in the 1960s is abandoned hulks of ramshackle houses that were once the homes of marginal farmers. Although the rains have returned to the plains and the population of the dust-bowl states has begun to grow again, after declining during the thirties and forties, the new growth is principally in the cities, which are becoming industrialized. Midwestern farming—as foreshadowed in *The Grapes of Wrath*—has become a big, mechanized business.

Second, and happily, the greater number of migrants did not literally disappear. Although there were more deaths among them—especially of children—than a civilized people should find tolerable, most of the "Joads" survived their harrowing experiences. Third—unhappily—there is little evidence that they really learned from their experiences the lessons of cooperation that Steinbeck hoped they and all men might. While the worst prophecies of the novel went unfulfilled, so did its best.

The migrant problem was actually on its way to solution

when Steinbeck's novel appeared. The height of the migration was 1936. The flood was stemmed thereafter by the notorious Los Angeles "border patrol," which turned back many migrants, who in turn warned others against attempting the trip. California also forcibly interfered with the migration by enforcing a statute that had been on the books since 1901. Section 2615 of the Welfare and Institutions Code of California read: "Every person, firm, or corporation or officer or agent thereof that brings or assists in bringing into the State any indigent person who is not a resident of the State, knowing him to be an indigent person, is guilty of a misdemeanor."

While the migration was kept in check, by methods of dubious legality, measures were taken to alleviate the conditions among those migrants who had managed to enter California. On September 1, 1937, Secretary of Agriculture Henry A. Wallace created the Farm Security Administration, as a successor to the old Resettlement Administration. By July 1941, when labor specialists began to anticipate a shortage of agricultural labor, the F.S.A. had set up thirty federal camps to care for more than fifteen thousand migrant families. Some cooperative farms had also been started in Arizona. The Supreme Court of the United States acknowledged the F.S.A.'s premise that "rural poverty is a national problem and must be coped with as a national problem" when, on November 24, 1941, it ruled California's "anti-migrant" law to be an "unconstitutional barrier to interstate commerce."

The law had already done its work, however, and by the time it was denounced by Associate Justice Robert H. Jackson as being "at war with the habit and custom by which our country has expanded," it was almost a dead letter. By

the autumn of 1941 California was worried not so much
about fending off surplus agricultural workers as by the
problem of providing facilities for the influx of workers to
the areas, especially around Los Angeles and San Diego,
where shipyards and defense plants were springing up. On
September 16, 1940, President Roosevelt had signed the
long and bitterly debated Compulsory Military Service
Law. Although farm workers were generally exempt from
the draft, the drafting of young men and the expansion of
defense industries to supply our own military needs and
those of friendly nations reduced the pool of surplus labor.
Then, only two weeks after the Supreme Court ruling on
the "anti-migrant" law, the United States was at war.

World War II, of course, accelerated the absorption of
the "Joads" into California's heterogeneous population.
Carey McWilliams has recalled, in a letter to the editor, this
process of absorption:

> During the war years I served as one of three members
> of a board of arbitration at the North American Aviation
> plant. It was quite apparent even then, listening to the
> witnesses in the various hearings, that the dust-bowl mi-
> grants were being pretty effectively absorbed and assim-
> ilated. In some cases, I was amused to note that even the
> accents began to disappear.
> Also, in the San Joaquin Valley, towns, many of which
> had so-called "little Oklahomas" on their outskirts in the
> mid-1930s, actually incorporated these shack-towns in
> their normal growth and development so that the shack-
> town itself was absorbed and became part of the larger
> community.

Another situation resulting from our entry into the war
increased the demand for agricultural labor in California.
On March 3, 1942, Lieutenant General John L. DeWitt,

Western Defense Commander of the United States Army, set aside an area of approximately a quarter of a million square miles as "a military zone from which all Japanese, American citizens as well as aliens, must move." This controversial removal of the Nisei (American citizens of Japanese descent) from more than half of Washington, Oregon, and California, and the irrigated farmlands of Arizona, uprooted many diligent and frugal Oriental farmers from carefully tended and highly productive farms that certain California patriots were suspected of coveting (prejudice was certainly shown by removing only Germans and Italians who were aliens from the military zone). This uprooting of some hundred thousand persons—including many farm workers—intensified the demand for agricultural workers to such an extent that in the same year the recruiting of "braceros"—Mexican nationals imported temporarily to work under contract in the fields—was authorized as a wartime emergency program. By 1943, only four years after the appearance of *The Grapes of Wrath*, a special California legislative committee was appointed to investigate the shortage of agricultural workers and to find means of obtaining additional seasonal workers in order to forestall a harvest crisis.

Persons close to the situation, including the national Congressional committee on the utilization of manpower headed by Representative John H. Tolan of California, as well as officials of the Department of Agriculture, predicted, nevertheless, that the problem of the "Joads" would arise again—perhaps in intensified form—after peace and demobilization. Even Steinbeck was wrong in supposing that the migrants who had grown up close to the soil would insist on remaining farmers. In fact, many of them shared the attitude of one of his "villains," Connie Rivers, who abandoned Rose-of-Sharon Joad and their unborn child in order to seek work as a mechanic; these remained with the defense-prompted industries that took permanent root along the Pacific Coast. Indeed the once alarming stream of migrants was but a trickle compared to the vast flood of new citizens that poured into California after the war and set it on the way to becoming our most populous state. The once sedentary agricultural giant of the West Coast has become an industrial giant and has shown an amazing capacity for absorbing the middle-class "Joads" lured by the promise of sunshine. Although the migratory-labor problem persists in California, as elsewhere, the problem of surplus population has shifted from the booming West Coast to some of the Eastern states, where mines and factories are being closed down because of industries moving, for example, to California.

The shocking and sobering lesson that we can still learn from the story of the Joads is that the real causes of the crisis of the late thirties were prejudice and hysteria. The native population's traditional distrust of the "outlander" combined with a lack of faith in the nation's future productive capacity to precipitate shameful events. The attitude of the Californians toward the "Joads" is epitomized by the bitterly contemptuous remarks addressed by the counsel for the state of California to the Supreme Court during the hearing on the "anti-migrant" law:

> A social problem in the South and Southwest for over half a century, the "poor white" tenants and share croppers following reduction of cotton planting, drought, and adverse conditions for small-scale farming, swarmed into California. . . . Should the states that have so long

tolerated, and even fostered, the social conditions that have reduced these people to their state of poverty and wretchedness, be able to get rid of them by low relief and insignificant welfare allowances and drive them into California to become our public charges, upon our immeasurably higher standard of public services? Naturally, when these people can live on relief in California better than they can by working in Mississippi, Arkansas, Texas or Oklahoma, they will continue to come to this state. [*United States Reports*, Volume 314.]

With influential persons holding this attitude, it is no wonder that it took a war to settle the "Joad" problem; but war as a "cure" is surely worse than the disease. If what Californians spent on trying to eliminate the migrants had been spent on caring for them temporarily, and if the thought that went into angry legal and extra-legal maneuvers had been devoted to planning for the future, the state's handling of the migrant problem might have afforded a model of how to cope with emergency conditions during a period of social transition, rather than a horrible example.

Those who believe that survival alone is enough can find a comforting answer to the question, "What became of the Joads?" Generally, they did survive, and some of them prospered. Those who with Steinbeck, however, seek something more than survival, must ruefully acknowledge that the best answer to the question is that the circumstances of war converted the "Joads" into Californians, which is what they had wanted to be all along—quite possibly of the very sort depicted in *The Grapes of Wrath* as fighting against the migrants' coming into the state.

PART II

Reception

CHAPTER 5

How Was The Grapes of Wrath *Received at Home?*

I

The Grapes of Wrath DID NOT HAVE A LONG ADVANCE build-up. It was first announced in the December 31, 1938 issue of *Publishers' Weekly*, only two and a half months before publication. Yet so great was the excitement over Steinbeck and the touchy question of the migrants that when the novel appeared on March 14, 1939, there had already been three advance printings. Fifty thousand copies were on order, and it had been necessary to halve all the orders so as to supply every dealer with copies before publication. A total of 19,804 copies bore the distinctive imprint and yellow top-stain of the first printing of this American classic.

Remarkably in an era when the national economy was still lagging and bargain buying flourished, *The Grapes of Wrath* achieved this record advance sale without the help of the influential book clubs. It had been selected as a monthly premium by the Book Union, but this organization apparently ceased to operate before the novel appeared, as trade records do not list any later selections. Nor did the advance sale do more than whet the public's appetite for the book. By April 29, when it first appeared on *Publishers'*

Weekly's list of national best-sellers, it was selling at the rate of 2500 copies a day and a total sale of 250,000 was predicted. By May 6 it had moved to the top of the best-seller list and was selling at the rate of nearly 10,000 copies a week.

The Viking Press admitted that none of its previous publications had sold at such an astonishing rate. It doubled the advertising appropriation on the book and ordered two extra carloads of paper simply to fill further orders for Steinbeck's novel. By May 17, 83,361 copies had been shipped and the publishers announced a contest among booksellers, who were to guess the total number of copies that would be shipped by the end of the year. Guesses averaged 349,612, although the actual number was close to 430,000.

In November the book was selling faster than it had been six months earlier—at the rate of over 11,000 copies a week. After being the top best-seller of 1939, *The Grapes of Wrath* remained one of the ten best-sellers of 1940. So popular was the original edition (then $2.75) even ten months after its publication that when the motion picture based on the book was released, in January 1940, no special "tie-in" edition was deemed necessary. For a limited time, however, the Literary Guild—which had missed a chance to offer the book as a selection—was allowed to distribute a special printing as a premium. This offer was discontinued, however, when a new "price-protected" edition of the novel appeared in May 1940.

Since then the novel has remained continuously in print. The regular trade edition (whose price, after two decades, had risen to $6) was supplemented by a two-volume special edition, with illustrations based on woodcuts by the distinguished midwestern artist Thomas Hart Benton, which was distributed to members of the Limited Editions Club —a group that prides itself on offering only outstanding classics of the past and present. The same illustrations were later used in a single-volume edition issued by the Heritage Club. The novel has also been reprinted in the Modern Library and by the Viking Press as a Compass Book, both retaining the pagination of the original edition. A second illustrated edition, with line drawings by John Garth, was for a time included in the Living Library, edited by Carl Van Doren; and the novel has proved, at various times and in several formats, one of the most popular titles in the Bantam paperback line. It would be almost impossible to compute the total sales of the American editions alone of this novel, which sells at a rate that would delight and profit the publishers of most brand-new fiction today.

There is a legend that the critical reception was equally and without exception enthusiastic; but this, like many legends, can be blasted by examining the pages of the periodicals of the time. The reviewers for the mass-circulation weeklies received the book with reservations. Although not hostile, they seemed determined not to be taken in by any publisher's propaganda. Trained as journalists and accustomed to reading rapidly and superficially, the weekly reviewers are best prepared to deal with novels that deftly manipulate standard formulas. They complained generally about the unconventional structure of *The Grapes of Wrath*.

Burton Rascoe wrote in *Newsweek* that the book was "beautiful and even magnificent," but "not well organized." "I can't quite see," he complained, "what the book is about, except that there are 'no frontiers left and no place to go' " —a matter that would in itself give most thoughtful persons serious pause. *Time*'s anonymous reviewer found the inter-chapters not "a successful fiction experiment," and though Clifton Fadiman, writing in *The New Yorker*, admitted that the novel "dramatizes so that you cannot forget it the terrible facts of a wholesale injustice committed by society," he complained that the latter half was "too detailed" and the folk note "forced a little."

Even the critics for the politically oriented liberal week-lies were not entirely pleased with the novel. Both Louis Kronenberger, writing in *The Nation*, and Malcolm Cowley, in *The New Republic*, were dissatisfied with the whole second half of the book and the ending in particular. Cowley did not think the book worthy to stand beside the best Hemingway and Dos Passos; and, although Kronen-berger found *The Grapes of Wrath* "in many ways the most moving and disturbing social novel of the time," he thought it "uneconomically proportioned." A more detailed com-plaint was delivered by Leon Whipple in the monthly *Survey Graphic*. Although he considered the book the work of a "first-rate novelist," he cautioned that the risk of confusing the reader about the difference between the real and the invented is "inherent in social novels." To help forestall such confusion, he made the somewhat unaesthetic proposal that "some philanthropist" commission "a popular interpreter of social events to digest the Senate Report ['Unemployment and Relief' by Professor Paul S. Taylor of the University of California] into a readable booklet with pictures, and provide a copy for every reader of *The Grapes of Wrath*."

Reviewers for the monthlies and the literary quarterlies— who were less concerned with the novel as sociology and had more time to consider its merits as art—were far more impressed by it and recognized its merits as a bold artistic experiment, carving out rather than following a trail.

Edward Weeks, editor of *The Atlantic Monthly*, considered *The Grapes of Wrath* "the summation of eighteen years of realism . . . a novel whose hunger, passion, and poetry are in direct answer to the angry stirring of our conscience these past seven years." Although he thought that the novel might be "if anything . . . too literal, too unsparing," he said he could "only hope that the brutality dodgers will take my word for it that it is essentially a healthy and disciplined work of art."

John Chamberlain in *Harper's* found it "a wise and tender and moving book as well as a social document of the first order," which showed Steinbeck to be almost the only exception to the regrettable lack of power among contemporary writers. Chamberlain had the advantage of knowing at first-hand the scenes of the novel and of having at one time been tempted to become a fruit-picker himself in California's lush valleys. His own experience enabled him to testify that "Steinbeck is the only [novelist] who has caught the predicament of an agrarian folk who have not changed with industry, or grown up in the paradoxes of industry." The depth and perspicuity of Chamberlain's comment make it apparent how important the critic's own experience may be in enabling him to come to terms with a trail-blazing work of art. The lukewarm reception of Steinbeck's work by some of the genteel critics could easily be due to their wider acquaintance with literature than with life.

The most effective answer to those who found fault with the structure of the novel was provided by Charles Angoff, writing in the dying *North American Review*. Angoff began with the most unequivocal praise the novel had yet received from a disinterested literary judge: "With his latest novel, Mr. Steinbeck at once joins the company of Hawthorne, Melville, Crane, and Norris, and easily leaps to the forefront of all his contemporaries. The book has all the earmarks of something momentous, monumental and memorable." He then answered directly those who had been fretted by the novel's language and construction: "The book has the proper faults: robust looseness and lack of narrative definiteness—faults such as can be found in the Bible, *Moby Dick*, *Don Quixote*, and *Jude the Obscure*. The greater artists almost never conform to the rules of their art as set down by those who do not practice it."

Though most of the early critics of the book were reluctant to commit themselves—perhaps until they had had an opportunity to see which way the winds of taste would blow—an exception was provided by reviewers in the Sunday book section of the two most influential New York newspapers. Peter Monro Jack, writing in *The New York Times Book Review*, said that "the real truth is that Steinbeck has written a novel from the depths of his heart with a sincerity seldom equalled." But the review that best sums up the most intelligent and most sympathetic early reaction to the book was that in *Herald Tribune Books* by Joseph Henry Jackson, reprinted in the following pages. Book editor of the *San Francisco Chronicle* and himself the author of a number of books about the colorful aspects of California's history, Jackson had followed Steinbeck's career long and sympathetically. His remains one of the most sensitive appraisals of Steinbeck's purpose and achievement that has appeared anywhere. Besides reviewing the novel, he was also chosen to write the Introduction to the special Limited Editions Club edition of the work.

Joseph Henry Jackson
The Finest Book John Steinbeck Has Written

"You never been called 'Okie' yet? . . . Okie us' ta mean you was from Oklahoma. Now it . . . means you're scum. Don't mean nothing itself, it's the way they say it. But I can't tell you nothin. You got to go there. I hear there's three hundred thousan' of our people there—an' livin' like hogs, 'cause ever'thing in California is owned. They ain't nothin' left. And them people that owns it is gonna hang on to it if they got ta kill ever'body in the worl' to do it. An' they're scairt, an' that makes 'em mad. You got to see it. You got to hear it. Purtiest goddamn country you ever seen, but they ain't nice to you, them folks. They're so scairt an' worried they ain't even nice to each other."

That was the tale told to the Joad family, tractored out of the red-earth-and-gray-dust country of Oklahoma and headed for California in a groaning jalopy for which they had paid almost their last cent. They had seen fine printed handbills telling them that California needed pickers for fruit, for peas, for cotton. Work for thousands; that was what those notices said. And the Joads, tractored, blown, swept off the land on which they and their family had lived for years, were on their way to find out. They were strong; all they wanted was a job. They were willing to work, every last one of them, even Ma and the children. Surely they would find an opportunity in California. Maybe they could even lay by a little and have a nice house. With four or five men, all working, it wouldn't be so hard to do.

Now there was this fellow who had been to California, meet-

From *The New York Herald Tribune Books*, April 16, 1939, p. 3. Reprinted by permission of the *New York Herald Tribune*.

ing them on the road, talking like that. Yet there was nothing to do but go on. There was no home to go back to. The bank had taken over, and a tractor had run a four-mile furrow right through their dooryard. Just in case they might be slow about moving out, the tractor had nudged the house, too, twisted it off its foundations, warped and cracked the walls, left it wrecked like Joad's dream. But the driver had a wife and children, and he needed the $3 a day. The bonus for "accidentally" wrecking the house would buy his older child a pair of shoes, too. There was nothing anybody could have done. And there was nothing to do now but drive on to California, like the thousands behind them and ahead of them.

Multiply the Joads by thousands and you have a picture of the great modern migration that is the subject of this new Steinbeck novel which is far and away the finest book he has yet written. Examine the motives and the forces behind what happened to the Joads and you have a picture of the fantastic social and economic situation facing America today. Cure? Steinbeck suggests none. He puts forward no doctrine, no dogma. But he writes, "in the souls of the people the grapes of wrath are filling and growing heavy, growing heavy for the vintage." I have no doubt that Steinbeck would not enjoy being called a prophet. But this novel is something very like prophecy.

The Joads were only one family to learn that a bank was not a man. It was made up of men, but it was a bigger thing and it controlled them, even though sometimes they hated to do what the bank-monster said they must. That monster moved out the Joads and other thousands. Little farms, even tenant-farming, wouldn't work any more on the worn-out land. Only huge land companies and tractors could make it pay. It happened all at once, and they had to go somewhere; thousands and tens of thousands were in the same boat.

Angry and puzzled, the heads of families tried to figure. When the little handbills appeared in the lost country, they thought they saw a way out. If they sold everything, they might buy an ancient car and move to California where the handbills said there was a chance for pickers. The second-hand car dealers cheated them right and left, but they bought the rattle-traps; they had to. And they took to the road, headed westward over Highway 66.

All along the road there sprang up little camps. In them there was death and birth, even laughter sometimes, and always there was the common dream—the dream of a future where there was enough work and where a man might save a little money, buy a piece of land, raise enough to feed his folks, hold up his head again. They were Americans, these people; Americans for seven generations back. They weren't afraid of work. They would get along.

So the Joads and the thousands of the dispossessed came to the promised land. And they learned what they had been brought there for. There was work, yes, in the pears, in the almonds, in the prunes and the peaches and the cotton. The handbills were right. But what the handbills hadn't explained was that when there were too many workers then wages could be forced down. Pay five cents a box for peach picking where there were starving men who would work for four, or three or even two and a half? We're paying two and a half cents. Take it or leave it. There's a thousand other men want the work. If you don't want it, then move along. Keep moving. And better not mention "decent wages." That's Red talk. There's deputies with guns and pick-handles for Reds. Keep moving. Take it or leave it. Who cares about a bunch of dirty Okies?

What happened to the Joads is the immediate story of this novel. What happened and is happening to the thousands like them is the story behind the story, the reason Steinbeck wrote *The Grapes of Wrath*. What may happen—must happen, he believes—in the long run is the implication behind the book. "Whereas the wants of the Californians were nebulous and un-defined, the wants of the Okies were beside the roads, lying there to be seen and coveted; the good fields with water to be dug for, earth to crumble in the hand, grass to smell. . . . And a homeless, hungry man, driving the roads with his wife [beside] him and his thin children in the back seat, could look at the fallow fields which might produce food but not profit, and that man could know how a fallow field is a sin and the unused land a crime against the thin children." There is the hint. And here again: "And the great owners, with eyes to read history, and to know the great fact: when property accumulates in too few hands it is taken away. And that companion fact: when a majority of people are hungry and cold they will take by force what they need. And the little screaming fact that sounds through history: repression works only to strengthen and knit the repressed." Prophecy, perhaps. Certainly a warning.

For the story itself, it is completely authentic. Steinbeck knows. He went back to Oklahoma and then came west with the migrants, lived in their camps, saw their pitiful brave highway communities, the life of the itinerant beside the road. He learned what was behind the handbills. And he came back with an enormous respect for the tenacity of these dispossessed, and with the knowledge that this migration is no less a forerunner of a new way than was that migration of those earlier Americans who took California from another group of landholders who had grown too soft to hold it.

It is a rough book, yes. It is an ineffably tender book too. It is the book for which everything else that Steinbeck has written was an exercise in preparation. You'll find in it reminders of *Pastures of Heaven,* of *In Dubious Battle,* of *The Red Pony,* even of *Tortilla Flat.* But here there is no mere exploration of a field, no tentative experimenting with a theme. This is the full symphony. Steinbeck's declaration of faith. The terrible meek will inherit, he says. They will. They are on their way to their inheritance now, and not far from it. And though they are the common people, sometimes dirty people, starved and suppressed and disappointed people, yet they are good people. Steinbeck believes that too.

It is easy to grow lyrical about *The Grapes of Wrath*, to become excited about it, to be stirred to the shouting point by it. Perhaps it is too easy to lose balance in the face of such an extraordinarily moving performance. But it is also true that the effect of the book lasts. The author's employment, for example, of occasional chapters in which the undercurrent of the book is announced, spoken as a running accompaniment to the story, with something of the effect of the sound track in Pare Lorentz's *The River*—that lasts also, stays with you, beats rhythmically in your mind long after you have put the book down. No, the reader's instant response is more than quick enthusiasm, more than surface emotionalism. This novel of America's new disinherited is a magnificent book. It is, I think for the first time, the whole Steinbeck, the mature novelist saying something he must say and doing it with the sure touch of the great artist.

II

The early reviews may have been equivocal, but there was no doubt about the enthusiasm for the book on the part of those awarding annual prizes for literary achievement. At a book-and-author luncheon at the Hotel Astor on February 13, 1940, reviewer Harry Hansen announced that members of the American Booksellers Association had chosen *The Grapes of Wrath* as their favorite novel of 1939 (the award for the "most original" novel went to Dalton Trumbo's bitter anti-war tract *Johnny Got His Gun*). Steinbeck received from the booksellers an engraved bronze paperweight in the form of an open book.

On April 1, 1940, it was announced during an intermission at the *Social Work Follies of 1940* that *The Grapes of Wrath* had received the first annual award of *Social Work Today*, a publication of the Social Service Employees' Union, for "individual work which has interpreted most effectively unmet social and economic need." A bronze statue accompanied this award.

When the *Saturday Review of Literature* conducted a "pre-Pulitzer" poll of American newspaper and magazine book reviewers, in its issue of May 11, 1940, thirty-eight out of fifty joined the editorial staff of the magazine in nominating *The Grapes of Wrath* as "the most distinguished novel of the year." (Even the Pasadena, California, critic joined the majority. Not the man from Los Angeles, however. San Francisco was unrepresented.) On May 6, 1940, the Trustees of Columbia University echoed the choice of the critics by announcing that the Pulitzer Prize for the year's most distinguished novel had indeed gone to *The Grapes of Wrath*. Steinbeck handed the thousand-dollar prize on to Richard Lovejoy of Monterey, to start the young department-store worker on a literary career.

One critic polled by the *Saturday Review of Literature* who did not select *The Grapes of Wrath* as the year's outstanding novel was Kenneth C. Kaufman of Oklahoma City's *Daily Oklahoman*. While Kaufman may have had other reasons for dissenting from the majority opinion, he may also have been influenced by local prejudice, for Steinbeck's novel was not warmly received in the state where its action begins. Indeed it aroused great hostility in both Oklahoma and California.

The course of California's agitated response to Steinbeck's handling of a controversial contemporary problem has unfortunately not been recorded. On August 23, 1939, according to *Publishers' Weekly*, the Kern County Board of Supervisors banned *The Grapes of Wrath* in the schools and libraries under its jurisdiction. The Associated Farmers of this embattled county (whose seat—Bakersfield—is unflatteringly depicted in Chapter Twenty of the novel) were also reported to have begun mapping a state-wide campaign to exclude both Steinbeck's book and Carey McWilliams' *Factories in the Field* from publicly supported institutions on the grounds that they "distorted the facts," but their efforts aroused little enthusiasm even in neighboring Fresno County. Prominent Californians generally kept out of the controversy over the novel, although Governor Culbert L. Olson spoke his piece in *Look* magazine (January 16, 1940). *The Commonweal* preserved in "Red Meat and Red Herrings" (October 13, 1939) a few scattered reactions: the San Bernardino *Sun*'s was unfavorable ("The fallacy of this should hardly be dignified by denial, it is so preposterous"), while that of the *East Bay Labor Journal* of Oakland was, not surprisingly, favorable ("a terrific exposure of the inhuman treatment of migratory workers by California employers").

The response of the Oklahomans was less inhibited, and was scrupulously set down at the time by a dispassionate and witty scholar, Martin Staples Shockley, whose "The Reception of *The Grapes of Wrath* in Oklahoma" is reprinted here as the most detailed account, drawn from fugitive sources, of the response to Steinbeck's novel in one of the states that found it most distasteful.

Martin Staples Shockley
The Reception of The Grapes of Wrath *in Oklahoma*

Most of us remember the sensational reception of *The Grapes of Wrath* (1939), Mr. Westbrook Pegler's column about the

From *American Literature*, XV (May 1944), 351-361. Reprinted by permission of the author and the Duke University Press.

vile language of the book, Raymond Clapper's column recommending the book to economic royalists, Mr. Frank J. Taylor's article in the *Forum* attacking factual inaccuracies, and the editorial in *Collier's* charging communistic propaganda. Many of us also remember that the Associated Farmers of Kern County, California, denounced the book as "obscene sensationalism" and "propaganda in its vilest form," that the Kansas City Board of Education banned the book from Kansas City libraries, and that the Library Board of East St. Louis banned it and ordered the librarian to burn the three copies which the library owned. These items were carried in the Oklahoma press. The *Forum*'s article was even reprinted in the Sunday section of the Oklahoma City *Daily Oklahoman* on October 29, 1939, with the editor's headnote of approval.

With such publicity, *The Grapes of Wrath* sold sensationally in Oklahoma bookstores. Most stores consider it their best-seller, excepting only *Gone With the Wind*. One bookstore in Tulsa reported about one thousand sales. Mr. Hollis Russell of Stevenson's Bookstore in Oklahoma City told me, "People who looked as though they had never read a book in their lives came in to buy it."

Of thirty libraries answering my letter of inquiry, only four, including one state college library, do not own at least one copy of the book, and the Tulsa Public Library owns twenty-eight copies. Most libraries received the book soon after publication in the spring of 1939. Librarians generally agreed that the circulation of *The Grapes of Wrath* was second only to that of *Gone With the Wind*, although three librarians reported equal circulation for the two books, and one (Oklahoma Agricultural and Mechanical College) reported *The Grapes of Wrath* their most widely circulated volume. The librarians often added that many private copies circulated widely in their communities, and some called attention to the extraordinary demand for rental copies. A few libraries restricted circulation to "adults only." About half the libraries mentioned long waiting lists, Miss Sue

Salmon of the Duncan Public Library reporting that "Even as late as the spring of 1940 we counted 75 people waiting." Mrs. Virginia Harrison of A. and M. College stated that the four copies there "were on waiting list practically the entire time up to March 19, 1941." After over two hundred students had signed the waiting list for the two copies in the University of Oklahoma library, faculty members donated several additional copies to the library.

The Grapes of Wrath was reviewed throughout Oklahoma to large and curious audiences. A high-school English teacher wrote that he had reviewed the book three times, at a ladies' culture club, at a faculty tea, and at a meeting of the Junior Chamber of Commerce, receiving comments ranging from one lady's opinion that Ma Joad was a "magnificent character," to a lawyer's remark that "such people should be kept in their place." When Professor J. P. Blickensderfer reviewed the book in the library at the University of Oklahoma, so many people were turned away for lack of standing room that he repeated the review two weeks later, again to a [capacity] audience.

Much of what has passed in Oklahoma for criticism of *The Grapes of Wrath* has been little or nothing more than efforts to prove or disprove the factual accuracy of Steinbeck's fiction. One of the minority supporters of the truth of Steinbeck's picture of the Okies has been Professor O. B. Duncan, head of the Department of Sociology at A. and M. College. In an interview widely printed in Oklahoma newspapers, Professor Duncan discussed the economic and social problems which are involved.

The farm migrant as described in Steinbeck's *Grapes of Wrath,* Duncan said, was the logical consequence of privation, insecurity, low income, inadequate standards of living, impoverishment in matters of education and cultural opportunities and a lack of spiritual satisfaction.

"I have been asked quite often if I could not dig up some statistics capable of refuting the story of *The Grapes of Wrath,*" Duncan related. "It cannot be done, for all the available data prove beyond doubt that the general impression given by Steinbeck's book is substantially reliable." [Oklahoma City *Times,* February 5, 1940.]

Billed as "the one man, who above all others, should know best the farm conditions around Sallisaw," Mr. Houston Ward, county agent for Sequoyah County, of which Sallisaw is the county seat, spoke over radio station WKY in Oklahoma City on March 16, 1940, under the sponsorship of the State Agriculture Department. Under the headline "Houston B. Ward 'Tells All' about *The Grapes of Wrath,*" the press quoted Mr. Ward on these inaccuracies:

Locating Sallisaw in the dust bowl region; having Grandpaw Joad yearning for enough California grapes to squish all over his face when in reality Sallisaw is one of the greatest grape-growing regions in the nation; making the tractor as the cause of the farmer's dispossession when in reality there are only 40 tractors in all Sequoyah county. . . . "People in Sequoyah county are so upset by these obvious errors in the book and picture, they are inclined to overlook the moral lesson the book teaches," Ward said.

Numerous editorials in Oklahoma newspapers have refuted or debunked Steinbeck by proving that not all Oklahomans are Joads, and that not all Oklahoma is dust bowl. The following editorial, headed "Grapes of Wrath? Obscenity and Inaccuracy," is quoted from the Oklahoma City *Times,* May 4, 1939:

How book reviewers love to have their preconceived notions about any given region corroborated by a morbid, filthily-worded novel! It is said that *Grapes of Wrath* by John Steinbeck, shows symptoms of becoming a best seller, by the kindness of naive, ga-ga reviewers. It pictures Oklahoma with complete and absurd untruthfulness, hence has what it takes. That American literary tradition is still in its nonage . . . is amply proved by the fact that goldfish-swallowing critics who know nothing about the region or people pictured in a novel accept at face value even the most inaccurate depiction, by way of alleged regional fiction. No, the writer of these lines has not read the book. This editorial is based upon hearsay, and that makes it even, for that is how Steinbeck knows Oklahoma.

Mr. W. M. Harrison, editor of the Oklahoma City *Times,* devoted his column, "The Tiny Times," to a review of the book on May 8, 1939. He wrote:

Any reader who has his roots planted in the red soil will boil with indignation over the bedraggled, bestial characters that will give the ignorant east convincing confirmation of their ideas of the people of the southwest. . . . If you have children, I'd advise against leaving the book around home. It has *Tobacco Road* looking as pure as Charlotte Bronte, when it comes to obscene, vulgar, lewd, stable language.

Usually the editors consider the book a disgrace to the state, and when they do not deny its truth they seek compensation. The editor of the Oklahoma City *Times* wrote on December 5, 1939:

Oklahoma may come in for some ridicule in other states because of such movie mistakes as *Oklahoma Kid* and such literature as the current *Grapes of Wrath.* Nationally we may rank near the bottom in the number of good books purchased, and in the amount we pay our teachers. But when the biggest livestock and Four H club show comes along each year the nation finds out that somebody amounts to something in Oklahoma.

On September 25, 1941, during the Oklahoma State Fair, the *Daily Oklahoman,* of Oklahoma City, carried a large cartoon showing the Oklahoma farmer proudly and scornfully reclining atop a heap of corn, wheat, and pumpkins, jeering at a small and anguished Steinbeck holding a copy of *The Grapes of Wrath.* The caption: "Now eat every gol-durn word of it."

Considerable resentment toward the state of California was felt in Oklahoma because California had stigmatized Oklahoma by calling all dust-bowl migrants—even those from Arkansas and Texas—"Okies." One lengthy newspaper editorial was headed "So California Wants Nothing But Cream" and another "It's Enough to Justify a Civil War." On June 13, 1939, the *Daily Oklahoman* carried under a streamer headline a long article on the number of Californians on Oklahoma's relief rolls. In Tulsa, employees of the Mid Continent Petroleum Company organized the Oklahoma's California Hecklers Club, the stated purpose being to "make California take back what she's been dishing out." The club's motto was "A heckle a day will keep a Californian at bay." A seven-point program was adopted, beginning, "Turn the other cheek, but have a raspberry in it," and ending, "Provide Chamber of Commerce publicity to all Californians who can read." The Stillwater *Gazette* in editorial approval wrote of the club, "*The Grapes of Wrath* have soured and this time it's the Californians who'll get indigestion."

Numerous letters from subscribers have appeared in newspapers throughout Oklahoma. Some are apologetic, some bitter, some violent. A few have defended Steinbeck, sympathized with the Joads, and praised *The Grapes of Wrath*. Some take the book as a text for economic, social, or political preachments. Miss Mary E. Lemon, of Kingfisher, wrote to the Oklahoma City *Times*:

> To many of us John Steinbeck's novel, *The Grapes of Wrath*, has sounded the keynote of our domestic depression, and put the situation before us in an appealing way. When the small farmers and home owners—the great masses upon which our national stability depends—were being deprived of their homes and sent roaming about the country, knocking from pillar to post; when banks were bursting with idle money, and insurance companies were taking on more holdings and money than they knew what to do with, Steinbeck attempted a sympathetic exposition of this status.

Mr. P. A. Oliver, of Sallisaw, wrote no less emphatically to the home town *Democrat-American* (March 28, 1940):

The Grapes of Wrath was written to arouse sympathy for the millions of poor farmers and tenants who have been brought to miserable ruin because of the development of machinery. . . . The people are caught in the inexorable contradiction of capitalism. As machinery is more and more highly developed, more and more workers are deprived of wages, of buying power. As buying power is destroyed, markets are destroyed. As the millions of workers are replaced by machinery in the industrial centers, the markets over the world collapse. The collapse of world markets destroyed the market for the cotton and vegetables produced by the poor farmers and tenants of Sequoyah county. Sequoyah county is a part of the world and hence suffered along with the rest of the capitalistic world in the collapse of capitalistic business. The day of free enterprise is done. The day of the little farmer is done. Had it not been for government spending, every farmer in the United States, every banker, every lawyer, every doctor, and all other professional workers and wage earners would long since have joined the Joads on the trail of tears. Better do some serious thinking before you ridicule the Joads.

From September 22 to 25, 1940, a Congressional committee headed by Representative Tolan of California held hearings in Oklahoma's capitol investigating the problem of migratory workers. Apparently Oklahoma viewed this intrusion with suspicion, for as early as August 16, an editorial in the *Payne County News* (Stillwater) stated that

Anticipating an attempt to "smear" Oklahoma, Governor Phillips is marshaling witnesses and statistics to give the state's version of the migration. He has called on Dr. Henry G. Bennett and faculty members of the Oklahoma A. and M. College to assist in the presentation. Oklahoma has a right to resent any undue reflections on the state. If the hearing develops into a mud-slinging contest, Oklahoma citizens have a few choice puddles from which to gather ammunition for an attack on the ham-and-egg crackpot ideas hatched on the western coast.

On September 9 the *Daily Oklahoman* of Oklahoma City carried a story giving the names of the members of the committee which the governor had appointed to prepare his report. The paper stated that "Governor Phillips announced his intention to refute the 'Okies' story when the committee of congressmen come here to study conditions causing the migration." During the hearings, front-page stories kept Oklahomans alert to Steinbeck's guilt. On September 20 the *Daily Oklahoman* reported with apparent relief that "the fictional Joad family of *The Grapes of Wrath* could be matched by any state in the union, according to testimony." Next morning the same paper's leading editorial on "Mechanized Farms and 'Okies' " stated that mechanized farming was not responsible for conditions represented in *The Grapes of Wrath*. The editorial concluded, "It is a disagreeable fact, but one that cannot be ignored by men earnestly seeking the truth wherever found, that two of the chief factors that produce 'Okies' are A.A.A. and W.P.A."

Under the heading " 'Grapes' Story Arouses Wrath of Governor," the *Oklahoma City Times* on October 2, 1939, printed the story of a correspondence between His Excellency Leon C. Phillips, governor of Oklahoma, and an unnamed physician of Detroit, Michigan. The unnamed physician wrote, as quoted in the paper:

> "Is it at all conceivable that the state of Oklahoma, through its corporations and banks, is dispossessing farmers and share-croppers . . . ? I am wondering whether you, my dear governor, have read the book in question." To which the governor warmly replied: "I have not read the thing. I do not permit myself to get excited about the works of any fiction writer. In Oklahoma we have as fine citizens as even your state could boast. . . . I would suggest you go back to reading detective magazines. . . ."

The following news item is quoted from the Stillwater *Gazette* of March 23, 1940:

Thirty-six unemployed men and women picketed Oklahoma's state capitol for two hours Saturday calling on Governor Phillips to do something about conditions portrayed in John Steinbeck's novel, *The Grapes of Wrath*. One of their signs stated "Steinbeck told the truth." Eli Jaffee, president of the Oklahoma City Workers' alliance, said, "We are the Okies who didn't go to California and we want jobs." Phillips refused to talk with the group. He said that he considered that the novel and movie version of the book presented an exaggerated and untrue picture of Oklahoma's tenant-farmer problem as well as an untruthful version of how migrants are received in California.

If His Excellency the Governor had been reticent as a critic of literature, the Honorable Lyle Boren, Congressman from Oklahoma, was no way abashed. The following speech, reprinted from the *Congressional Record*, was published in the *Daily Oklahoman*, January 24, 1940:

Mr. Speaker, my colleagues, considerable has been said in the cloakrooms, in the press and in various reviews about a book entitled *The Grapes of Wrath*. I cannot find it possible to let this dirty, lying, filthy manuscript go heralded before the public without a word of challenge or protest.

I would have my colleagues in Congress, who are concerning themselves with the fundamental economic problems of America know that Oklahoma, like other states in the union, has its economic problems, but that no Oklahoma economic problem has been portrayed in the low and vulgar lines of this publication. As a citizen of Oklahoma, I would have it known that I resent, for the great state of Oklahoma, the implications in that book. . . .

I stand before you today as an example in my judgment, of the average son of the tenant farmer of America. If I have in any way done more in the sense of personal accomplishment than the average son of the tenant farmer of Oklahoma, it has been a matter of circumstance, and I know of a surety that the heart and brain and character of the average tenant farmer of Oklahoma cannot be surpassed and probably not equaled by any other group.

Today, I stand before this body as a son of a tenant farmer, labeled by John Steinbeck as an "Okie." For myself, for my dad and my mother, whose hair is silvery in the service of building the state of Oklahoma, I say to you, and to every honest, square-minded reader in America, that the painting Steinbeck made in his book is a lie, a black, infernal creation of a twisted, distorted mind.

Some have blasphemed the name of Charles Dickens by making comparisons between his writing and this. I have no doubt but that Charles Dickens accurately portrayed certain economic conditions in his country and in his time, but this book portrays only John Steinbeck's unfamiliarity with facts and his complete ignorance of his subject. . . .

Take the vulgarity out of this book and it would be blank from cover to cover. It is painful to me to further charge that if you take the obscene language out, its author could not sell a copy. . . .

I would have you know that there is not a tenant farmer in Oklahoma that Oklahoma needs to apologize for. I want to declare to my nation and to the world that I am proud of my tenant-farmer heritage, and I would to Almighty God that all citizens of America could be as clean and noble and fine as the Oklahomans that Steinbeck labeled "Okies." The only apology that needs to be made is by the state of California for being the parent of such offspring as this author. . . .

Just nine days after Congressman Boren's speech had appeared in print, a long reply by Miss Katharine Maloney, of Coalgate, appeared on the "Forum" page of the *Oklahoma City Times*. I quote a few brief excerpts from Miss Maloney's letter:

If Boren read *The Grapes of Wrath*, which I have cause to believe he did not, he would not label John Steinbeck a "damnable liar." John Steinbeck portrayed the characters in his book just as they actually are. . . . Why, if Boren wants to bring something up in Congress, doesn't he do something to bring better living conditions to the tenant farmer? . . . This would make a better platform for a politician than the book. . . .

Not only politics but the pulpit as well were moved by the book. One minister in Wewoka was quoted as praising it as a "truthful book of literary as well as social value, resembling in power and beauty of style the King James version of the Bible." His was decidedly a minority opinion. The other extreme may be represented by the Reverend W. Lee Rector, of Ardmore, who considered *The Grapes of Wrath* a "heaven-shaming and Christ-insulting book." As reported in the press, the Reverend Mr. Rector stated:

"The projection of the preacher of the book into a role of hypocrisy and sexuality discounts the holy calling of God-called preachers. . . . The sexual roles that the author makes the preacher and young women play is so vile and misrepresentative of them as a whole that all readers should revolt at the debasement the author makes of them." The pastor complained that the book's masterly handling of profanity tends to "popularize iniquity" and that the book is "100 percent false to Christianity. We protest with all our heart against the Communistic base of the story. . . . As does Communism, it shrewdly inveighs against the rich, the preacher, and Christianity. Should any of us Ardmore preachers attend the show which advertises this infamous book, his flock should put him on the spot, give him his walking papers, and ask God to forgive his poor soul."

Other Oklahomans resented the filming of the story. Mr. Reo M'Vickn wrote the following letter, which was published in the *Oklahoma City Times* on January 26, 1940:

After reading the preview of *Grapes of Wrath* (*Look,* January 16) I think the state of Oklahoma as a whole should take definite steps to prevent the use of the name of our state in such a production. They are trying to disgrace Oklahoma and I for one am in favor of stopping them before they get started.

Oklahoma Chambers of Commerce had already tried to stop the filming of the picture. The following story is taken from the *Oklahoma City Times,* August 7, 1939:

> Neither Stanley Draper, secretary-manager of the Oklahoma City Chamber of Commerce, nor Dr. J. M. Ashton, research director of the State Chamber of Commerce, wants Twentieth Century-Fox Corporation to make *Grapes of Wrath* in the "dust bowl." . . . Enough fault was found with the facts in Joseph [*sic*] Steinbeck's book on the "okies." . . . So the two Chamber of Commerce men think someone should protest the inaccurate and unfair treatment the state seems to be about to receive in the filming of the picture. Draper is going to suggest the mayor of Oklahoma City protest, and Ashton will ask the governor to do likewise. . . .

On September 1, 1941, the *Daily Oklahoman* carried a four-column headline, "Lions to Attack 'Okie' Literature." The news story described the nature of the attack:

> Those who write smart and not so complimentary things about Oklahoma and Okies had better watch out, because the 3-A district governor of Oklahoma Lions clubs and his cabinet, at their first session here Sunday, discussed an all-out counter-offensive. . . . The district governor and a dozen members of his cabinet agreed in their meeting at the Skirvin Hotel that something should be done to offset *Grapes of Wrath* publicity. . . .

The opinions and incidents which I have presented are representative, by no means inclusive. There are, I should say, two main bodies of opinion, one that this is an honest, sympathetic, and artistically powerful presentation of economic, social, and human problems; the other, the great majority, that this is a vile, filthy book, an outsider's malicious attempt to smear the state of Oklahoma with outrageous lies. The latter opinion, I may add, is frequently accompanied by the remark, "I haven't read a word of it, but I know it's all a dirty lie."

The reception of *The Grapes of Wrath* in Oklahoma suggests many interesting problems particularly pertinent to contemporary regional literature in America. Any honest literary interpretation of a region seems to offend the people of that region. Ellen Glasgow, though herself a Virginian, was received in her native state with a coolness equal to the warmth with which Virginians welcomed Thomas Nelson Page. Romanticizers of the Old South are local literary lions, while authors who treat contemporary problems are renegades who would ridicule their own people for the sake of literary notoriety.

A tremendous provincial self-consciousness expresses itself in fierce resentment of "outsiders who meddle in our affairs." One consistent theme in the writings of Oklahomans who attacked *The Grapes of Wrath* was that this book represents us unfairly; it will give us a lot of unfavorable publicity, and confirm the low opinion of us that seems to prevail outside the state. Rarely did someone say, "We should do something about those conditions; we should do something to help those people." Generally they said, "We should deny it vigorously; all Oklahomans are not Okies."

Properly speaking, *The Grapes of Wrath* is not a regional novel; but it has regional significance; it raises regional problems. Economic collapse, farm tenantry, migratory labor are not regional problems; they are national or international in scope, and can never be solved through state or regional action. But the Joads represent a regional culture which, as Steinbeck shows us, is now rapidly disintegrating as the result of extra-regional forces. It may well be that powerful extra-regional forces operating in the world today foreshadow the end of cultural regionalism as we have known it in America.

III

The irate Oklahomans received some spasmodic support in their efforts to suppress the book, but it was not banned even in traditionally censorious Boston. In fact, the first published reports of trouble did not appear until August 12, 1939, when Dr. Alexander Galt, public librarian of Buffalo, New York, was described in *Publishers' Weekly* as refusing to purchase the novel because "standards of life needed" normally "should be higher than in this book." Through Quincy Howe, the National Council of Freedom from Censorship protested Dr. Galt's action, but the protest was unavailing: the peppery librarian pointed out that he had not banned the book, but simply refused to buy it. The American Civil Liberties Union reported that other, unpublicized librarians had done the same.

The novel was specifically banned for the first time on grounds of "obscenity" by the Kansas City, Missouri, Board of Education, but few groups followed its lead. One sensational episode (mentioned by Mr. Shockley in his article) occurred, however, when on November 21, 1939, the Library Board of East St. Louis, Illinois, ordered three token copies of the novel burned. This order was compared by enraged liberals all over the country with the barbarous tactics of the Nazis, then much in the news. After a stormy session, attended by some members who had been absent from the meeting that had ordered the burning, the board by a vote of 6-2 rescinded the order and ordered instead that the novel be shelved as "for adults only." According to the St. Louis, Missouri, *Globe-Democrat,*

The shift in the Board's position took place after a spirited debate. . . . John Maher, one of the members favoring the ban, questioned the sociological value of the book and is quoted as saying, "These people cannot be helped and will not be helped, so reading the book won't help any." Mrs. W. H. Matlack, the other opponent of the book, a prominent local clubwoman, said that the book "is vile all the way through." She added, "Its historical value has been disproved. *Gone With the Wind* had historical value."

But the admirers of the book rallied a much more distinguished woman than Mrs. Matlack to their cause. The best answer to those who have sought to suppress the novel or to minimize its value appeared on June 28, 1939, in Mrs. Eleanor Roosevelt's syndicated column, "My Day":

Now I must tell you that I have just finished a book which is an unforgettable experience in reading. *Grapes of Wrath* by John Steinbeck both repels and attracts you. The horrors of the picture, so well drawn, made you dread sometimes to begin the next chapter, and yet you cannot lay the book down or even skip a page. Somewhere I saw the criticism that this book was anti-religious, but somehow I cannot imagine thinking of "Ma" without, at the same time, thinking of the love "that passeth all understanding."

The book is coarse in spots, but life is coarse in spots, and the story is very beautiful in spots just as life is. We do not dwell upon man's lower nature any more than we have to in life, but we know it exists and we pass over it charitably and are surprised how much there is of fineness that comes out of baser clay. Even from life's sorrows some good must come. What could be a better illustration than the closing chapter of this book?

CHAPTER 6

Was The Grapes of Wrath *Answered?*

THE EARLY REVIEWERS OFTEN COMPARED *The Grapes of Wrath* to *Uncle Tom's Cabin*. Certainly the two books were alike in focusing attention upon a national disgrace and in provoking cries of outrage from those who felt themselves maligned. The Associated Farmers of California and Chambers of Commerce in Oklahoma railed as vehemently against Steinbeck as dedicated Southerners had against Mrs. Stowe.

The sensationally successful anti-slavery novel prompted a series of book-length "answers," among them Mrs. Mary Eastman's *Aunt Phillis's Cabin; or, Southern Life As It Is*, and Robert Criswell's *"Uncle Tom's Cabin" Contrasted with Buckingham Hall, the Planter's Residence; or, A Fair View of Both Sides of the Slavery Question*, presenting the "other side" of the picture. These led the authoress to publish, the year after her novel, a "Key" documenting the charges that she had made in it. Several such "answers" to Steinbeck's novel were published, but they were not widely circulated at the time and less than twenty years later have become rare books.

The Associated Farmers of California at one time announced that they were preparing a documented reply to Steinbeck's "distortions of fact," to be called "Plums of

Plenty," but no work bearing this title ever appeared. The burden of response fell instead on a few enthusiastic but ill-equipped individuals, among them one George Thomas Miron, who—perhaps inspired by David's conquest of Goliath—directed against the 619-page novel a 26-page pamphlet, *The Truth about John Steinbeck and the Migrants,* which was offered for sale from a Los Angeles post-office box address.

Miron professed to have lived—like Steinbeck—among the migrants in California's valleys and to have followed the harvest with them. He reported that he had had no difficulty in finding work and that he had seen many migrants turn down jobs in order to accept relief. The general tone of his argument is conveyed by a paragraph describing the migrants:

> Like anywhere else in American life, of course, it was always very apparent that the enterprising, the ambitious, the energetic, the higher-grade citizens, were making their way while the other kind were not doing so well. That relief and social workers find it is among the poorest classification of migratory workers where the most ill-health and unemployment prevails was proved to be true by a survey made by the Council of Women for Home Missions. A typical report from a group of churches, as quoted by Edith E. Lowry, the Council's Executive Secretary, describes the migrant families where the most distressing conditions prevailed in these words, "The migrant families were decidedly low-grade and illiterate."

Much of Miron's "truth" is an unsupported denunciation of the novelist as a Leftist. One finishes the pamphlet, however, wondering just where Miron disagrees with Steinbeck, for his last paragraph reads:

And one soon learned that many of the migratory families are of good pioneer stock, asking nothing more than
that they have a chance to work, a chance to get back
on a piece of land of their own, and no longer to be the
subjects for continual controversy, or guinea pigs for
laboratory experiments of left-wing visionaries.

This is precisely what Steinbeck had been arguing ever
since he published his stories on the migrant camps in the
San Francisco News. One suspects that to Miron a "Red"
is not one who adopts a position on ideological grounds,
but one who—as the canner Hines says in *The Grapes of
Wrath*—"wants thirty cents an hour when we're payin'
twenty-five!"

Much the same arguments as Miron advances underlie
another pamphlet, *Grapes of Gladness: California's Refresh-
ing and Inspiring Answer to John Steinbeck's "The Grapes
of Wrath"* by Marshal V. Hartranft, published in Los
Angeles in 1939. Hartranft was presumably the author of
an earlier pamphlet with a similarly mouth-filling title, *The
Dollar Crop and the History of Its Manipulation by the
Corporate Money Power in Conspiracy against the Amer-
can People* (Sacramento, 1896). His indisputable thesis in
Grapes of Gladness is that "if everybody knew how to
take a living direct from the resources of the earth like
the California Indian did, we would never hear anything
about want or hunger." To illustrate his claim that "California still has room for any who can feed themselves from
our endless-chain gardens, instead of from the State Treasury," Hartranft tells the story of Shore Acres, a suburban
real-estate development where migrants are given an acre of
land to work in return for minimal payments of interest and
taxes. At the end of his narrative, a dispossessed Midwestern
family that has been lucky enough to discover this para-

dise rides—in the best Western tradition—to the rescue of some of the pitiful specimens Steinbeck describes in his novel.

Again it is hard to see just how this pamphlet "answers" *The Grapes of Wrath*, since Hartranft agrees with Steinbeck that the migrants should be given an opportunity to re-establish themselves as independent, small-scale farmers. Steinbeck's "error," it becomes apparent from Hartranft's "Addenda Analyzing 'The Grapes of Wrath,'" is that he proposes to help even those who are not what a Salvation Army captain calls "the right kind of folks"—those recommended by home-town clergymen and businessmen. Hartranft does not say what is to be done with those "folks" who are not "the right kind"; presumably they are to be pushed into the Pacific.

Actually the greatest value of Hartranft's pamphlet lies not in his anachronistic reconstruction of what Henry Nash Smith in *Virgin Land* calls "the myth of the garden" (the notion that a Western agricultural paradise settled by sturdy, independent yeomen would be the dominant force in American society), but in a document he appends which sets forth the views of Steinbeck's most vigorous California opponents—the Citizens Association of Bakersfield. This statement is reprinted in its entirety in the following pages as an illustration of the provincial self-righteousness that first drove Steinbeck to write his novel and then condemned him for doing so.

Miron's and Hartranft's answers to Steinbeck were obviously assembled hurriedly. A much more impressive answer, though indirect, came from Mrs. Ruth Comfort Mitchell (in private life Mrs. William Sanborn Young, of Los Gatos, California), who had published more than a dozen volumes of poetry and sentimental fiction; much of her writing appeared originally in *The Woman's Home Companion*. A dynamic leader in professional women's groups, Mrs. Mitchell appeared just the person to place the California agricultural situation in its proper light before respectable readers. She attempted to do so in a novel, *Of Human Kindness* (1940), in which, without mentioning Steinbeck or his book by name, she glorifies the struggle of a proud and independent California farm family to wrest a living from the soil, and attributes the problems posed by the "Okies" to the shiftlessness of the migrants and the agitation of over-sexed Communists. Unfortunately, the "Okies" Mrs. Mitchell portrays are not comparable to Steinbeck's Joads; the only migrant to play a prominent role in her fable is a Gene Autry-like cowboy singer who comes from a respectable Oklahoma family and who admits that he has come West simply out of an urge to roam. The implication seems to be that the whole vast westward migration from the dust bowl was simply a lark, carried out by romantic drifters.

Carey McWilliams, author of *Factories in the Field*, contributed a devastating review of Mrs. Mitchell's novel to *The New Republic*, reprinted here with McWilliams' reply —printed in a later issue of the same magazine—to a letter from Edward L. Smith of the D. Appleton-Century Company (Mrs. Mitchell's publisher), who had irately denied that her novel was intended as a reply to Steinbeck's. This exchange appears to have ended the ineffectual efforts to "answer" *The Grapes of Wrath*. Steinbeck was never obliged to compile the kind of "key" to the book that Mrs. Stowe did for *Uncle Tom's Cabin*, although, in *Their Blood Is Strong*, he had provided one even before writing his novel.

California Citizens Association Report

Bakersfield, California, July 1, 1939

Despite optimistic announcements of a decline in the number of migrants coming to California principally from Oklahoma, Arkansas, Texas, and Missouri, the burden on the taxpayers of our state has become more acute. It is now that the local and state relief rolls are being filled with artificially created "residents," subsidized by the Farm Security Administration for the year's required eligibility. It is now that we are feeling the financial pressure of building new schools for the migrants' children.

It is *now* that we are paying.

Records of the Kern County Hospital show that 44 per cent of the patients taken care of there during the past year were nonresidents, and the origin of 77 per cent of that number was in the four states mentioned. In this period more than 110,000 cases were treated free.

These migrants are not farmers who have been dispossessed. Even the Farm Security Administration, which once claimed evidence to the contrary, now admits that they were either sharecroppers or laborers in their home states. It is plain that there was no place for them here when there were already five unemployed for every available agricultural job in California.

Even in the potato fields of Kern County there were dozens of people for every job, and that is true also of the other crops. In face of this fact, most of the migrants have been living on public bounty since coming to California.

The reduction in acreage in all branches of agriculture and the necessary proration to keep the industry from disaster are such as to limit labor needs. The migration came at the time when it was utterly impossible to give employment to additional

This document is reprinted as it appears in *Grapes of Gladness*, by Marshall V. Hartranft (Los Angeles: De Vorss, 1939), pp. 124-125.

workers without destroying the established farm economic system.

The United States Employment Service is authority for the fact that no effort was made by any California farm group to bring labor here, by advertising or any other means. The farmers neither needed nor wanted additional workers, nor did they want the tax cost of supporting unneeded migrants.

California has always maintained the highest farm wages of any area in the world, but it cannot continue to be oppressed by taxes to feed these surplus workers and still uphold this standard.

The author, John Steinbeck, in his novel, *Grapes of Wrath,* did great injustice both to Californians and to the migrants themselves. These hapless people are not moral and mental degenerates as he pictures them, but victims of desperate conditions —conditions which can bring to California the same tragedy that drove them from their home states.

The recounting by Steinbeck of incidents in which violence was used upon the transients is based upon nothing more than the envisionings of an over-worked imagination. It is absolutely untrue.

A deep-set prejudice seems to be the only explanation for the involving of the American Legion in a fictionally-created harassment of these people.

The California Citizens Association, made up of various organizations, presented to the Congress petitions signed by hundreds of thousands of people, directing the attention of the government to the fact that no further migration could be endured by the people of California. The record of the California Citizens Association has been one of sympathy for these people, but one that must now be tempered by a deep desire to maintain our standard of living and by the natural law of self-preservation.

—Thos. W. McManus, Secretary

Carey McWilliams

Glory, Glory, California

Shortly after *The Grapes of Wrath* was published, Mrs. Ruth Comfort Mitchell announced that she was hard at work on a "reply" that would deal with the migratory-labor problem in California "without kid gloves." Mrs. Mitchell then confirmed her militant intentions by presiding over a mammoth luncheon in San Francisco, devoted to the task of denouncing Mr. Steinbeck. Consequently her new book, *Of Human Kindness*, must be considered as a partisan document. Being a novel written in reply to another novel, it necessarily invites comparison with *The Grapes of Wrath*.

Of Human Kindness has to do with the Banners, a yeoman farm family of the San Joaquin Valley. Their daughter, Sally, runs away with a hired hand—"Lute," a dumb, shiftless, sex-tormented Okie with a taste for hill-billy music. The marriage of his daughter to an Okie is too much for Ed Banner, a two-fisted, hard-hitting son of the frontier. But alas, the daughter's aberrance is only the beginning of the domestic and social crisis that engulfs the Banner family. The son, Ashley, falls under the subversive influence of a Red on the faculty of the local high school, who looks "a little like a rabbit" and instructs her pupils that conditions in California are "just like the French Revolution." His mental balance disturbed by this incendiary talk, young Ashley throws in his lot with a girl Communist. "She's Carmen—and Delilah—and Borgia," screams Mary Banner, the heroine. "She's appalling. She terrifies me. She's a Black Widow Spider!" She is also, it seems, an enchantress. "Willow

From *The New Republic*, CIII (July 22, 1940), 125. This review, as well as Mr. McWilliams' letter to Edward L. Smith (page 142), which appeared in the "Correspondence" columns of *The New Republic*, CIII (September 2, 1940), 305, are reprinted here by permission of *The New Republic*.

slim in her white slacks and thin white sweater which was drawn down revealingly over her round little breasts," she hangs limp in the arms of agricultural workers, kisses them "lightly," and in a husky, throbbing voice whispers, "So long, Babe!" Poor Ashley Banner succumbs to the wiles of this cheap Communist whore, and follows her into the fields. But he soon discovers her in a rut with a Party organizer, and the spell that her insidious charm once exercised is forever broken.

Well, anyway, the story is sweetly resolved: Ashley returns home, penitent and reactionary, apologizes to Papa and nominates the Old Man for state senator; Sally, too, comes home with the no-good Okie and a baby; Ed Banner, in league with his fellow farmers—most of whom are described, incidentally, as small farmers operating eighty acres or so—drives the Reds from the community; "Pinky" Emory, the rabbit-like teacher, is bumped off; and Mary Banner, momentarily bewitched by a charming Eastern journalist who visits the Banners in order to get the real, honest-to-God lowdown on the migratory-labor problem, remains true to her husband and a great and beneficent calm descends upon the valley.

As one who writes and speaks on behalf of the Associated Farmers, Mrs. Mitchell is unable to describe trade-union organizers, Okies, liberal schoolteachers, and similar characters objectively. She has an obvious distaste for characters of this type and makes them out as a pretty low and detestable breed. But she does not do much better with her own people, the farmers, the townspeople, the first citizens. In her anxiety to become their partisan, she makes them out as sociological saints. The Associated Farmers are the kindest men imaginable—a little quick on the trigger, perhaps; a little brusque with their women-folk, but underneath their sun-tanned leathery hides, just the salt of the earth. They use force, yes, but it is benevolently applied: a few cracked skulls, a little blood, a few teeth knocked out; but no murders, no vigilantism, no mob violence. As for the living and working conditions of migratory farm labor in

California, Mrs. Mitchell makes it quite plain that certain un-named latecomers to California—"scolding jays and sharp-beaked butcher-birds"—have grossly misrepresented the facts.

Now that the briefs have been filed, so to speak, for both sides, the public should be able to render a verdict. But *Of Human Kindness* and *The Grapes of Wrath* should not be read alone. There is still another document that should be studied, namely, the transcript of the La Follette Committee hearings in California, the volumes of which are now available. They give the facts without the fiction, and the facts support Mr. Steinbeck. As for Mrs. Mitchell's long-awaited reply, let's be kind to her and forget it.

LETTER TO EDWARD L. SMITH

Sir:

On December 8, 1939, as reported in the *Stockton Record* of that date, Mrs. Ruth Comfort Mitchell addressed the annual convention of the Associated Farmers of California, the topic of her speech being, "Her version of *The Grapes of Wrath*." Commenting on this talk, the *Pacific Rural Press* on December 16, 1939, stated: "Mrs. Young is writing a new book, *Of Human Kindness,* giving the other side of *The Grapes of Wrath,* which she dismisses as highly imaginative and sensational fiction." The "Mrs. Young" referred to is Ruth Comfort Mitchell.

This same report quotes Ruth Comfort Mitchell as getting "a big laugh" when she said that she was "still waiting for a copy of one of those sinister orange-colored handbills." I have a number of the handbills in my office for inspection at any time, and quite recently the Farm Security Administration, in their San Francisco offices, turned up a number that they found in circulation—not in 1937 but in 1940.

The *Los Angeles Times* on June 28, 1939, carried an item to the effect that Ruth Comfort Mitchell had written a novel giv-ing "the ranchers' side of the migratory labor problem" and also quoted her to the effect that her novel would give "a different view of the problem than that presented by her neighbor, John Steinbeck."

The *Eureka* [California] *Times* of June 1, 1940, describes a function at which Ruth Comfort Mitchell, "speaking from a table decorated in red, white and blue" again took Mr. Steinbeck to task for having written *The Grapes of Wrath*.

The purpose of the Palace Hotel luncheon affair, as I said before, was to launch a counter-offensive against *The Grapes of Wrath*.

CAREY MCWILLIAMS

Los Angeles, Calif.

CHAPTER 7

How Has The Grapes of Wrath
Been Received Abroad?

THE PECULIARLY AMERICAN PROBLEMS WHICH *The Grapes of Wrath* depicts and the Southwestern dialect of its characters raise the question of how much appeal the novel has had outside this country. Has it been taken as merely another example of United States "local color" or regional art?

It may be answered that almost anything dealing with actual conditions in this country is read abroad with consuming interest. *The Grapes of Wrath* is regional, moreover, only in its setting; its theme of man's need to overcome his selfish drives and to learn to help others in need is universally applicable. Though the particular circumstances it pictures may not be familiar to readers in other countries, they can recognize the moral problems that lie at the heart of the book and respond to its author's plea for compassion.

Any doubts about Steinbeck's international appeal and reputation have been set to rest by his receiving the Nobel Prize for literature in 1962. Indeed the best testimony to his international standing came in the radio announcement of the award, made on October 25, 1962 by Dr. Anders Osterling, Permanent Secretary of the Swedish Academy and Chairman of the Nobel Committee of the Academy, in those parts* which deal with *The Grapes of Wrath* and Steinbeck's work as a whole:

This year's Nobel Prize for Literature has been awarded the American author John Steinbeck.

The now just sixty-year-old prize-winner was born in the little town of Salinas in California, a town lying a few miles from the Pacific Coast and near the fertile Salinas Valley, which forms the background to many of his descriptions of the everyday life of the common man. He was raised in moderate circumstances but on terms of equality with the workers' families in this motley and diversified district; he often had to earn his bread by taking temporary work on the ranches at the same time as he studied at Stanford University, where, however, he never graduated. In 1925 he went to New York to try to exist as a free-lance writer. He failed, and after some bitter years of struggle he returned to California, where he found a home in a lonely cottage by the sea and there continued his writing. He already had several books behind him when in 1935, with the story *Tortilla Flat*, he achieved a popular success for the first time. These spicy and comic tales are about a gang of *paisanos*, asocial individuals who, in their wild revels, in a burlesque fashion resemble King Arthur's Knights of the Round Table. It has been said that in the United States this book came as a welcome antidote against the gloom of the then prevailing Depression. The laugh, at one blow, was now on Steinbeck's side.

But he had no mind to be an unoffending comforter and entertainer. Instead, the topics he chose were serious and denunciatory, for instance the bitter strikes on California's fruit and cotton plantations, which he depicted in his novel *In Dubious Battle*. His literary power steadily gained in impetus during these years. The little master-

* Two paragraphs devoted to Steinbeck's most recent novel, *The Winter of Our Discontent*, are omitted from the statement.

piece *Of Mice and Men*, the story of Lennie, the imbecile giant, who out of tenderness alone squeezes the life out of every living creature that comes into his hands, was followed by those incomparable short stories which he collected together in the volume *The Long Valley*. The way had now been paved for the great work that is principally associated with Steinbeck's name, the epic chronicle *The Grapes of Wrath*, which tells of the migration to California forced upon a group of people from Oklahoma by unemployment and the abuse of power. This tragic episode in the social history of the U.S.A. has inspired in Steinbeck a poignant description of life as it is lived by the common man, a description centered on the experiences of one particular farmer and his family on the endless, heartbreaking journey to a new home. . . .

Among the masters of modern American literature who have already been awarded this prize—from Sinclair Lewis to Ernest Hemingway—Steinbeck more than holds his own, independent in position and achievement. There is in him a strain of grim humor which to some extent redeems his often cruel and crude motif. His sympathies always go out to the oppressed, the misfits, and the distressed; he likes to contrast the simple joy of life with the brutal and cynical craving for money. But in him we find the American temperament also expressed in his great feeling for nature, for the tilled soil, the waste land, the mountains and the ocean coasts, all an inexhaustible source of inspiration to Steinbeck in the midst of, and beyond, the world of human beings.

The Academy's reason for awarding the prize to John Steinbeck reads as follows: "For his at one and the same time realistic and imaginative writings, distinguished as they are by a sympathetic humor and a social perception."

Steinbeck's international reputation did not, however, like that of some Nobel Prize winners, arise solely from this honor. *The Grapes of Wrath* has been applauded throughout the world since its first publication. A British edition appeared only a few months after the American, and though England was by then at war the novel attracted wide attention. Within three months of its initial publication, arrangements had been made for its translation into Danish, Dutch, French, Italian, Norwegian, Polish, Portuguese, Romanian, Spanish, Swedish, and even Russian; the author had refused to grant permission for a German edition. Doubtless still other translations would have appeared at once, had not World War II broken out within six months of the novel's publication.

It would be impossible to recount here all the tribulations the novel incurred in its international publishing history because of wartime paper shortages and the Axis invasions of some of the countries in which American novels were most eagerly read. What happened to it in France during the war years, as told by two young Americans, Thelma M. Smith and Ward L. Miner, in *Transatlantic Migration* (1955), is perhaps typical. The distinguished French scholar Maurice Coindreau had begun even before the war, in collaboration with Marcel Duhamel, a translation entitled *Le Ciel en sa Fureur*, from the opening lines of La Fontaine's fable about the animals sick with the plague seeking a scapegoat. Their translation was not yet completed when the Germans overran France. The Germans, who according to Jean-Paul Sartre "tried to use pessimistic American books for propaganda purposes," urged the French publisher Gallimard to issue the novel during the Occupation; when Gallimard refused, a translation by a Belgian collaborator was prepared, under the title *Grappes d'Amertume*, for publication by the Franco-German Institute. Plans for promoting the novel were disrupted by the Normandy invasion. After the war, when Steinbeck's reputation in France was enormously high, owing largely to an "underground," war-time edition of *The Moon Is Down,* issued by the Resistance publisher Editions de Minuit, the Coindreau-Duhamel version of *The Grapes of Wrath* was rushed into print; the translators were obliged to use the literal rendering of the title that had become known during the war. From May to December 1946 the novel was serialized in the popular weekly *Les Lettres Françaises;* when it appeared in book form in 1947, it became the sixth-best-selling novel of the year, reaching to a total sale of approximately 120,000 copies.

With war-time publishing restrictions lifted, the novel became popular not only in most European countries but in Asia and Africa. New editions and translations continued to appear. In 1959 and 1960 alone, UNESCO reported new editions in Bulgaria, Denmark, Germany, Hungary, and South Korea. An Italian publisher even brought out a special twentieth-anniversary edition.

In most Western countries critics have discussed the novel in the same terms as Americans, and a mere listing of international reviews would add little to the account of its reception. Of special interest, however, both because of postwar tensions between the United States and Russia and because *The Grapes of Wrath* has been accused by some detractors of following the "party line," is the Russian reaction to the novel.

According to Deming Brown's *Soviet Attitudes toward American Writing* (1962), *The Grapes of Wrath* has had the greatest impact in Russia of any American novel about the Depression. Translations of parts of the book appeared in periodicals in 1940. These were followed in 1941 by an edition of 300,000 copies of the complete work, which

Brown says is "by far the largest single printing an American work had ever enjoyed in Russia."

Steinbeck is thus one of the few contemporary American authors to achieve popularity in the Soviet Union, although his work is obviously being exploited in that country as the Nazis had also hoped to exploit it—as evidence of American decadence and the imminent collapse of our system. That it does not lend itself to such exploitation, however, may be seen in Jean-Paul Sartre's statement (in *The Atlantic Monthly* in 1946) that in France such an uncompromising novel as *The Grapes of Wrath* "never disgusted us with America—on the contrary, we saw in it a manifestation of your liberty." The injustices that the novel exposes, Sartre wrote, "have never seemed to us a defect of American society but rather a sign of the imperfections of our times."

Steinbeck offers no more comfort to Russian than to American extremists, as is apparent from the conclusion of *A Russian Journal* (1948), his report of his visit to the Soviet Union in the summer of 1947:

> We know that this journal will not be satisfactory either to the ecclesiastical left, nor the lumpen right. The first will say it is anti-Russian, and the second that it is pro-Russian. Surely it is superficial, and how could it be otherwise? We have no conclusions to draw, except that Russian people are like all other people in the world. Some bad ones there are surely, but by far the greater number are very good.

Russian critics have, nonetheless, attempted to read Steinbeck's novel in a way that suited their own purpose. In a lecture delivered in Moscow in 1947 under the auspices of the Ministry of Higher Education, the speaker, M. Mendelson,* asserted that *The Grapes of Wrath* is "justly considered one of the greatest works of modern American literature." Although he called the work of such American writers as Faulkner, Henry Miller, Erskine Caldwell, Richard Wright, and William Saroyan "degenerate" and even labeled Steinbeck's *Cannery Row* as evidence of "an extraordinarily unhealthy state of mind," Mr. Mendelson paid this tribue to Steinbeck's earlier novel:

> *The Grapes of Wrath* was written by a man who understood clearly that existing American social conditions, and not their own natural shortcomings, were responsible for the Joads' fate. He knew, above all, that those to blame for the Joads' plight were men of a fascist bent who were willing to let those workers who had become superfluous to them die of hunger. The author of *The Grapes of Wrath* felt that the Joads were true representatives of American democracy, that they possessed lofty human qualities, a sense of their own individual dignity, and the capacity to struggle against oppression.

That the Soviet line has not changed since 1947 is demonstrated by a much more detailed consideration of the novel, part of a long critical essay on Steinbeck's artistic development by R. Orlova published in the Soviet literary journal *Inostrannaia Literatura (Foreign Literature)* in 1962, in an issue that also included a section from Steinbeck's new novel *The Winter of Our Discontent*. The excerpts from Miss Orlova's essay given here demonstrate the effects of applying Marxist literary doctrine to a modern classic. Her analysis is a remarkable illustration of the way in which an alien

* Quoted in *Soviet Interpretation of Contemporary American Literature* (Washington, D.C., Public Affairs Press, 1948), p. 18.

argument may be interpreted in terms of the "party line." The article also shows the availability of American critical works to Russian scholars; one wonders, in view of this, whether the occasional inaccuracies in the article should be attributed to careless scholarship or to deliberate misrepresentation.

R. Orlova

Money against Humanity: Notes on the Work of John Steinbeck

John Steinbeck is a deeply controversial writer, just as controversial as the reality by way of which he was formed. Creator of pages of high prose and of pages of third-rate reading, he is the author of deeply veracious books; master of the poetical, universal *Grapes of Wrath* and weak interpreter of the philosophical discordance of the twentieth century through fiction in *East of Eden*; thoughtful social critic and author of light-weight, "rose-colored," one-day pieces. These contradictions appear, to differing extents, in all his books.

Like the farmer—and equally vainly—he strives to retain his property, where he is the master, not dependent on anyone else. Steinbeck desires to create and to retain his own world, an independent and secluded world of unmutilated humanity, populated with singular and excellent people. His aspirations are, however, fruitless in the end; such a patriarchal world of simple human ties does not exist in America any more as it did of yore.

From *Inostrannaia Literatura* No. 3 (March 1962), pp. 197-208. Portions of this article dealing with *The Grapes of Wrath* have been translated from the Russian especially for this volume by Armin Moskovic. Quotations from *The Grapes of Wrath* are from the original American edition; Steinbeck's letters are quoted in the form in which they appear in Lewis Gannett's Introduction to *The Portable Steinbeck* (1946) and in *The Wide World of John Steinbeck* by Peter Lisca (1958).

Steinbeck depicts not only the results but the very process of the inexorable annihilation of his ideals. The source of the tragic quality and, at the same time, of the humanity in his creative work is that he does not accept the existing, established social order.

Money against humanity—here is the foundation of the new novel [*The Winter of Our Discontent*], the old but unaging collision that is the subject of American reality and American literature, the old but unaging subject that is the "leitmotif" of John Steinbeck's creative work. . . .

The Grapes of Wrath is dedicated "To Carol, who willed this book. To Tom, who lived it." The last words of this dedication could refer to the author himself. He was caught in the whirlpool of the class struggle. He went to Oklahoma, joined a group of squatters, made the entire trip to California with them. He says in one of his letters [to Lawrence Clark Powell]: "I have to write this sitting in a ditch. I'm out working—may go south to pick a little cotton. Migrants are going south now and I'll probably go along." He wanted to distribute the thousand dollars [a week] that he was supposed to get for the film rights to *Of Mice and Men* to his starving companions. When the magazine *Life* proposed that he write an essay about what he saw and experienced, Steinbeck wrote [his agents] that he could not accept a fee: "I'm sorry but I simply can't make money on these people. . . . The suffering is too great for me to cash in on it."

After having started work on the novel, he wrote to his publisher:* "I have to go over into the interior valleys. There are five thousand families starving to death over there, not just hungry but actually starving. . . . I've tied into the thing from the first and I must get down there and see it and see if I can do something to knock these murderers on the heads. . . . The death of children by starvation in our valleys is simply staggering. . . . I'll do what I can. . . . Funny how mean and how

* Actually to his agent, Elizabeth Otis.—Ed.

little books become in the face of such tragedies." He really did all he could, and his book was neither little nor petty.

The book grew from the revolt and indignation of an honest man who could not calmly look at hunger and injustice. His future heroes were at the beginning comrades in cot and barrack, in ditches and tents. This is how the best book of the author and one of the most significant American novels of the twentieth century had its origins.

The Grapes of Wrath stirred up violent polemics. The guardsmen of the status quo, of course, accused the writer of slander. . . .*

In the state of Kansas, *The Grapes of Wrath* was banned from libraries.** A judge in Buffalo declared, "This book is more dangerous than dynamite." Three copies were solemnly burned in the city of St. Louis.† At the same time striking workers were carrying posters with the words "Steinbeck has told the truth."

The book became a best-seller. Steinbeck was awarded the highest literary prize in the United States, the Pulitzer Prize. The book circulated far beyond the boundaries of California and the United States, although actually it is a book about Oklahomans in California in the middle thirties at the climax of the world economic crisis—a book that was deeply "attached" to the locality by thousands of unduplicatable threads, a fact which caused American critics frequently to regard it as an example of regional, provincial literature. It arose out of journalism; Steinbeck had previously published in the San

---

* There follows a long quotation from a speech delivered to the House of Representatives by Lyle Boren, Congressman from Oklahoma, which has already been quoted in Martin Staples Shockley's "The Reception of *The Grapes of Wrath* in Oklahoma" (page 125), which is probably Miss Orlova's source.—ED.

** This sentence probably refers to the banning in Kansas City, Missouri.—ED.

† Miss Orlova presumably refers here to the order of the Library Board of East St. Louis, Illinois, which was rescinded before it could be carried out.—ED.

Francisco *Chronicle** articles about the seasonal workers in California.

The book is also attached to the epoch; it was shaped not from cooled-down lava but from something that was on the newspaper pages, on everybody's lips—from what was the pain of that time.

The Joads were striving for the same thing that thousands of Americans were striving for: a little home and garden, one's own piece of land, the whole family together, and plenty of food. For Ma Joad this dream has the same incantatory power as for the homeless tramps Lennie and George [in *Of Mice and Men*]—a dream as natural and modest as it is unrealizable.

And these simple, rude people are presented in the complete ordinariness and commonness of their existence, but with a genuine tragic greatness, the greatness of saga, of the heroic epic, interwoven in the telling.

The author tells how man is straightening himself, how his life is becoming filled with a higher purpose, how he is realizing the truth that one must serve others. This truth is personified in different manners in the characters of Ma and Tom Joad and of the former preacher Casy.

The knowledge of human community, of calm renunciation and firmness, was born with Ma, as if it had been possessed for ages. Ma does not develop but reveals herself in the novel. Good, thrifty housewife, she displays outstanding endurance, force of spirit, courage. For some time she travels side by side with the corpse of her own mother,** silently and resignedly bearing her grief, not shifting to anyone else a grain of her burden. It is necessary to reach California and not to waste time upon the dead; it is necessary to keep silent and to suffer —necessary not for Ma herself, but for the entire family. Ma does not reproach anybody; she does not make sacrifices to anybody. She acts as she does because she cannot act otherwise.

* Actually the *News.*—ED.
** Actually her mother-in-law.—ED.

Ma Joad, direct descendant of those rough people who mastered the virgin continent, cut passages in thickets, hunted, sewed, cooked, washed. She does everything and carries that wonderful light of the family, which is not visible when present but which is so agonizingly missed when extinguished.

Ma is a good person; she regards kindness as of greater value than family property. After Tom's return from prison, she sternly inquires about his becoming embittered. As the family passes through one after another of the several circles of migratory hell, Ma fears more than anything else that those nearest to her may turn into those two-legged animals with which she has so often had to clash. The kindness of the mother is not all weakness. Because of the limitless goodness of her soul, she is a very proud person: "We're Joads. We don't look up to nobody. Grampa's grampa, he fit in the Revolution."

Tom does change in the course of the distress which has to be suffered. The son of his mother, he has returned from prison a good-natured man, longing greatly for peace, for quiet, for the secluded life he knew before imprisonment. Thinking is difficult for him; he is not used to it. But he cannot help asking questions; he cannot help seeking answers. Tom becomes a fighter, not because he is looking for a fight, but because without fighting it is impossible to remain a man.

Among Steinbeck's many enemies were the churchmen. They got mightily mad at the characterization of the preacher Casy, who realized the hypocrisies of his former profession and abandoned it. The selfless struggle of Casy, who became one of the organizers of a strike and was killed by a policeman, finally helps Tom and others besides Tom to choose their way. . . .*

The main hindrance on the way to that truly human society for which Ma and Tom and Casy strive is the bourgeois order. *The Grapes of Wrath* is a flaming and consistently anti-capitalistic book. In it the question is not of particular shortcomings

* A long quotation from Casy's last speeches follows.—ED.

of the system, but of its fundamental principles. The author says, "If you who own things people must have could understand this, you might preserve yourself. If you could separate causes from results, if you could know that Paine, Marx, Jefferson, Lenin, were results, not causes, you might survive. But that you cannot know. For the quality of owning freezes you forever into 'I,' and cuts you off forever from the 'we.' "

In all his books Steinbeck writes about people. He depicts naïve and giddy, reckless idlers, drunkards, women of ill repute. These traits are present in the Joads. He depicts the mass of strikers in *In Dubious Battle* as human beings brought to despair, angered, compelled to defend themselves against authorities. (It is interesting to note that the expression "grapes of wrath" first appears on the pages of the novel *In Dubious Battle*.) And these traits are present in the Joads. He saw people working in the open air, people merged with the earth, brawling and ribald. And these traits as well appear in the Joads.

It is relatively easy to find in *The Grapes of Wrath* that which connects this novel with Steinbeck's previous creative work. It is much more difficult to comprehend the miracle of the leap, the mysterious distinction between the Joads and other characters created by the author. This book will live because today's American unemployed see in the Joads' destiny their own, because hunger still exists in the land, because there are still regions where people are driven away from their land, where they are deceived by cunning politicians, because within America and beyond its boundaries exploitation of man by man still exists.

But *The Grapes of Wrath* lives and will live because of that active, deep humanism which is expressed in this book more powerfully than in other works of the writer: "The last clear definite function of man—muscles aching to work, minds aching to create beyond the single need—this is man." And this idea will also remain alive at the time when people eat bread sown by themselves and live in homes built by themselves.

The specifically historical and the universally human are manifest in the construction as well as in the style of the novel.

The Grapes of Wrath is the tale of the ordeal of the Joads—the seizure of their land by the bank, the purchase of the truck, the trip to California, the unsuccessful search for work, the break-up of the family; this tale is interrupted by chapters not having a direct relation to their story—the meditations of the writer, his observations, the description of drought in Oklahoma or of Highway 66, on which the rich and satiated speed along. These observations are made by the Joads with their own eyes, but are also made by the eyes of the author (the description of the highway is quite similar in content and style to the angry pages Hemingway wrote about the yacht owners in the novel *To Have and Have Not*). These chapters are not so much about the Joads as they are about Americans generally, about mankind, about the life of man on earth.

Of course, the historically specific in the novel is not exhausted with the history of the Joads, it is present also in the interpolated chapters; on the other hand, the Joads do exhibit above all else a sublimity common to all mankind.

This universal quality is evident also in the language of *The Grapes of Wrath*. Steinbeck has been subjected to much criticism because of the slang—the dialect in which his heroes speak, little understood outside Oklahoma—and the profanity with which the novel is colored. His heroes use the dialect of Oklahoma's declassed farmers of the middle thirties; but the development of images and ideas in the book demands also other language, so that side by side with the "low" arises also the "high" style of the book. The two styles are, of course, not separate, but joined by a great number of complex and controversial connections.

The high style of the book can be traced back to the Bible. The Bible is a unique book, read by many Americans for a century and a half at those times during which the national character was being formed and the foundations of a national culture laid. Biblical garments were in England and America the national dresses of the revolutionary struggle. The influence of the Bible has been and continues to be investigated by the majority of American writers.

Steinbeck artistically transformed the language of the Bible into part of the organic alloy called *The Grapes of Wrath.*

PART III

Reputation

CHAPTER 8

Is the Movie Like the Book?

ALTHOUGH KNOWING COLUMNISTS SUCH AS WHITNEY Bolton had predicted that Hollywood would ignore *The Grapes of Wrath*, Annie Laurie Williams, who handled motion-picture rights for Steinbeck's agents, announced on April 20, 1939, a week after the publication of the novel, that Darryl Zanuck of Twentieth Century-Fox had paid $75,000 for the film rights (the price was high, but not a record). Even after that skeptics doubted that the film would be made, and it was rumored that a bank had ordered Zanuck to buy the rights in order to shelve the work. It went into production, however, almost at once, with the innocuous title "Highway 66" serving as a cover.

So rapidly did director John Ford and his assistants go about their work that the film was given its world première, at the Rivoli Theatre in New York, on January 24, 1940, only nine months after the contract for the film had been signed—a remarkably short time for a major production. The film had been made so quickly that the book was still a national best-seller at the time of the première.

The picture found overwhelming approval with the critics. Frank S. Nugent in the *New York Times* wrote that the film was "just about as good as any picture has a right to be." Yet it was not simply the *succès d'estime* that some worrybirds had predicted. The *New York Times* reported on February 25, 1940, that the local first-run engagement alone was expected to return one-seventh of the $750,000 it was estimated to have cost (less than one-fifth the cost of *Gone With the Wind*).

The only seriously discordant note in the chorus of praise that attended the opening of the film was sounded in the exhibitors' trade journal, *Motion Picture Herald*, whose editor, Martin Quigley, protested against the movie's sordid subject matter, maintaining that "the entertainment motion picture is no place for social, political, and economic argument." Quigley—a co-author of the Hays Code—added naïvely that the conditions depicted were either untrue or a cause for immediate revolution. He was answered by a five-page defense of the film by editor Maurice Kann of the trade journal *Box Office*.

Widespread enthusiasm for a superior piece of moviemaking does not necessarily mean that the film in question is faithful to the book on which it is based. Many readers of *The Grapes of Wrath* have had an opportunity to judge this relationship for themselves, for the motion picture is one of the comparatively few commercial Hollywood films to be included, with distinguished foreign and experimental motion pictures, in the standard repertoire of the "film classics" that makes the rounds of American colleges and culturally-minded communities. Even those familiar with both novel and film, however, will find useful and provocative George Bluestone's discussion of the differences between the two, reprinted in the following pages. Drawing upon an analysis of the content of the two versions of *The Grapes of Wrath*, Bluestone deals in detail with the nature and significance of the changes made for the film. In the course of his account, Bluestone also provides one of the best analyses ever published of the artistic structure of the novel itself.

George Bluestone
Novel into Film: The Grapes of Wrath

In his compact little study of California writers, *The Boys in the Back Room*, Edmund Wilson comments on the problems inherent in the close affiliation between Hollywood and commercial fiction:

> Since the people who control the movies will not go a step of the way to give the script writer a chance to do a serious script, the novelist seems, consciously or unconsciously, to be going part of the way to meet the producers. John Steinbeck, in *The Grapes of Wrath,* has certainly learned from the films —and not only from the documentary pictures of Pare Lorentz, but from the sentimental symbolism of Hollywood. The result was that *The Grapes of Wrath* went on the screen as easily as if it had been written in the studios, and was probably the only serious story on record that seemed equally effective as a film and as a book.

Indeed, not only did Steinbeck learn from Pare Lorentz; he also received, through Lorentz, his first introduction to Nunnally Johnson, the screen writer who did the movie adaptation of his novel. And Bennett Cerf, the publishing head of Random House, must have had none other than Steinbeck in mind when he wrote in *Hollywood Reporter* (January 9, 1941), "The thing an author wants most from his publisher these days is a letter of introduction to Darryl Zanuck." For if Steinbeck was for-

From *Novels into Film*, by George Bluestone (Baltimore: the Johns Hopkins Press, 1957), copyright © 1957 by the Johns Hopkins Press. Chapter 5 (pp. 147-169) is reprinted here by permission of the Johns Hopkins Press. Footnotes in the original have been incorporated in the text.

tunate in having Pare Lorentz as a teacher and Nunnally Johnson as a screen writer, he was one of the few who earned the
coveted letter to Darryl Zanuck, the producer of *The Grapes of
Wrath.* Add Gregg Toland's photography, Alfred Newman's
music, and John Ford's direction, and one sees that Steinbeck
had an unusually talented crew, one which could be depended
upon to respect the integrity of his best-selling book.

Lester Asheim, in his close charting of the correspondence
between twenty-four novels and films, seems to corroborate
Edmund Wilson's conclusion about the easy transference of
Steinbeck's book to John Ford's film. According to Asheim's
analysis, the major sequences in the novel bear more or less
the same ratio to the whole as the corresponding sequences do
in the film:

	Per cent of whole	
Sequence	*Book*	*Film*
Oklahoma episodes	20	28
Cross-country episodes	19	22
General commentary	17	—
Government-camp episodes	15	18
Hooverville episodes	10	13
Strike-breaking episodes	9	16
Final episodes	10	3
	100	100*

And when Asheim goes on to explain that, if one ignores the
major deletions which occur in the transference and considers
only those episodes in the novel which appear in the film, the
percentage of both book and film devoted to these central events
would be virtually identical, his observation seems, at first, to
be providing indisputable proof for Wilson's claim.

Yet to follow through Wilson's primary analysis of Stein-

* This chart and the accompanying commentary derive from Lester
Asheim's unpublished Ph.D. dissertation, "From Book to Film"
(University of Chicago, 1949).

beck's work is to come at once on a contradiction which belies, first, his comment on the ineluctable fitness of the novel for Hollywood consumption and, second, his implication that Steinbeck, like the novelists whom Bennett Cerf has in mind, had written with one eye on the movie market. For it is central to Wilson's critical argument that the "substratum which remains constant" in Steinbeck's work "is his preoccupation with biology." According to Wilson's view, "Mr. Steinbeck almost always in his fiction is dealing either with the lower animals or with human beings so rudimentary that they are almost on the animal level." Tracing the thematic seams that run through Steinbeck's prose, Wilson notes the familiar interchapter on the turtle whose slow, tough progress survives the gratuitous cruelty of the truck driver who swerves to hit it. This anticipates the survival of the Joads, who, with the same dorsal hardness, will manage another journey along a road, emerging like the turtle from incredible hardships surrounded by symbols of fertility, much like the turtle's "wild cat head" which spawns three spearhead seeds in the dry ground. And Wilson notes, too, the way in which the forced pilgrimage of the Joads, adumbrated by the turtle's indestructibility, is "accompanied and parodied all the way by animals, insects and birds," as when the abandoned house where Tom finds Muley is invaded by bats, weasels, owls, mice, and pet cats gone wild.

This primary biological analysis seems to contradict Wilson's more casual statement on the film, since the screen version, as evolved by Nunnally Johnson and John Ford, contains little evidence of this sort of preoccupation. And when Asheim concludes, after a detailed comparison, that to one unfamiliar with the novel there are no loose ends or glaring contradictions to indicate that alterations have taken place, we begin to uncover a series of disparities which, rather than demonstrating the ease of adaptation, suggests its peculiar difficulties. We are presented in the film with what Asheim calls "a new logic of events," a logic which deviates from the novel in several important respects.

Tracing these mutations in some detail will illuminate the special characteristics of book and film alike. The question immediately arises, how could *The Grapes of Wrath* have gone on the screen so easily when the biological emphasis is nowhere present?

Undeniably, there is, in the novel, a concurrence of animal and human life similar to that which appears in the work of Walter Van Tilburg Clark, another western writer who transcends regional themes. Even from the opening of the chapter which depicts the pedestrian endurance of the turtle, creature and human are linked:

> The concrete highway was edged with a mat of tangled, broken, dry grass, and the grass heads were heavy with oat beards to catch on a dog's coat, and foxtails to tangle in a horse's fetlocks, and clover burrs to fasten in a sheep's wool; sleeping life waiting to be spread and dispersed, every seed armed with an appliance of dispersal, twisting darts and parachutes for the wind, little spears and balls of tiny thorns, and all waiting for animals and for the wind, for a man's trouser cuff or the hem of a woman's skirt, all passive but armed appliances of activity, still, but each possessed of the anlage of movement.

Here, the central motifs of the narrative are carefully but inobtrusively enunciated, a kind of generalized analogue to the coming tribulations of the Joads: a harsh, natural order which is distracting to men and dogs alike; a hostile, dry passivity which, like the dormant blastema, is at the same time laden with regenerative possibilities. From the opening passages ("Gophers and ant lions started small avalanches. . . .") to the last scene in which an attempt is made to beatify Rose of Sharon's biological act, the narrative is richly interspersed with literal and figurative zoology. Tom and Casy witness the unsuccessful efforts of a cat to stop the turtle's slow progress. In the deserted house, Muley describes himself as having once been "mean like a wolf," whereas now he is "mean like a weasel." Ma Joad describes the law's pursuit of Pretty Boy Floyd in animal terms: "they run him like a coyote, an' him a-snappin' an' a-snarlin', mean as a lobo." Young Al boasts that his Hudson jalopy will "ride like a bull calf." In the interchapter describing the change, the growing wrath triggered by the wholesale evictions of the tenant farmers, the western states are "nervous as horses before a thunder storm."

Later, Ma Joad savagely protests the break-up of the family: "All we got is the family unbroke. Like a bunch of cows, when the lobos are ranging." Later still, Tom tells Casy that the day he got out of prison he ran himself down a prostitute "like she was a rabbit." Even the endless caravans of jalopies are described in terms which echo the plodding endurance of the turtle. After a night in which "the owls coasted overhead, and the coyotes gabbled in the distance, and into the camp skunks walked, looking for bits of food," the morning comes, revealing the cars of migrants along the highway crawling out "like bugs." After the relatively peaceful interlude of the government camp, Al comments on the practice of periodically burning out the Hoovervilles where the dispossessed farmers are forced to cluster: ". . . they jus' go hide down in the willows an' then they come out an' build 'em another weed shack. Jus' like gophers." And finally, toward the end, Ma expresses her longing to have a settled home for Ruth and Winfield, the youngest children, in order to keep them from becoming wild animals. For by this time, Ruth and Winnie do, indeed, emerge from their beds "like hermit crabs from shells."

The persistence of this imagery reveals at least part of its service. In the first place, even in our random selections, biology supports and comments upon sociology. Sexual activity, the primacy of the family clan, the threat and utility of industrial machinery, the alienation and hostility of the law, the growing anger of economic oppression, the arguments for human dignity, are all accompanied by, or expressed in terms of, zoological images. In the second place, the presence of literal and figurative animals is more frequent when the oppression of the Joads is most severe. The pattern of the novel, as we shall see, is similar to a parabola whose highest point is the sequence at the government camp. From Chapter Twenty-two to the middle of Chapter Twenty-six, which covers this interlude, the animal imagery is almost totally absent. Densely compacted at the beginning, when Tom returns to find his home a shambles, it recurs in the closing sequences of the strike-breaking and the flood.

The point is that none of this appears in the film. Even the highly cinematic passage depicting the slaughtering of the pigs, in preparation for the journey, is nowhere evident in the final editing. If the film adaptation remains at all faithful to its original, it is not in retaining what Edmund Wilson calls the constant substratum in Steinbeck's work. It is true, one may argue, that biological functions survive in the Joads' elementary fight for life, in the animal preoccupation with finding food and shelter, in the scenes of death and procreation, but this is not what Edmund Wilson has in mind. In the film, these functions are interwoven so closely with a number of other themes that in no sense can the biological preoccupation be said to have a primary value. This type of deletion could not have been arbitrary, for, as Vachel Lindsay showed as early as 1915 in *The Art of the Moving Picture,* animal imagery can be used quite effectively as cinema. Reviewing Griffith's *The Avenging Conscience,* Lindsay is describing the meditations of a boy who has just been forced to say good-by to his beloved, supposedly forever. Watching a spider in his web devour a fly, the boy meditates on the cruelty of nature: "Then he sees the ants in turn destroy the spider. The pictures are shown on so large a scale that the spiderweb fills the end of the theater. Then the ant-tragedy does the same. They can be classed as particularly apt hieroglyphics. . . ." More recently, the killing of the animals by the boy in *Les Jeux Interdits* [*Forbidden Games*] shows that biology can still effectively support cinematic themes. In the particular case of *The Grapes of Wrath*, however, the suggestions of the book were abandoned. If, then, we are to understand the mutation, to assess the film's special achievement, we must look elsewhere.

Immediately, a number of other motifs strongly assert themselves in Steinbeck's model: the juxtaposition of natural morality and religious hypocrisy; the love of the regenerative land; the primacy of the family; the dignity of human beings; the socio-political implications inherent in the conflict between individual work and industrial oppression. Consider Casy's impulsive rationalizations in the very early section of the book where he tries, like the Ancient Mariner, to convince his listener and himself at the same time that his rejection of religious preaching in favor of a kind of naturalistic code of ethics is morally acceptable. Tortured by his sexual impulses as a preacher, Casy began to doubt and question the assumptions which he had been articulating from his rough, evangelical pulpit, began to observe the discrepancy between theoretical sin and factual behavior. He repeats his conclusions to Tom, "Maybe it ain't a sin. Maybe it's just the way folks is. Maybe we been whippin' hell out of ourselves for nothin'. . . . To hell with it! There ain't no sin and there ain't no virtue. There's just stuff people do. It's all part of the same thing. And some of the things folks do is nice, and some ain't nice, but that's as far as any man got a right to say."

Casy retains his love for people, but not through his ministry, and later this love will be transmuted into personal sacrifice and the solidarity of union organization. This suspicion of a theology not rooted in ordinary human needs continues to echo throughout the novel. When Casy refuses to pray for the dying Grampa, Granma reminds him, quite offhandedly, how Ruthie prayed when she was a little girl: " 'Now I lay me down to sleep. I pray the Lord my soul to keep. An' when she got there the cupboard was bare, an' so the poor dog got none.' " The moral is clear: in the face of hunger, religious piety seems absurd. After Grampa's death the inclusion of a line from Scripture in the note that will follow him to his grave is parodied in much the same way, but Casy's last words at the grave echo his earlier statement: "This here ol' man jus' lived a life an' jus' died out of it. I don't know whether he was good or bad, but that don't matter much. He was alive, an' that's what matters. An' now he's dead, an' that don't matter . . . if I was to pray, it'd be for the folks that don' know which way to turn." Ma Joad expresses the same kind of mystical acceptance of the life cycle when she tries to tell Rose of Sharon about the hurt of childbearing:

> "They's a time of change, an' when that comes, dyin' is a piece of all dyin', and bearin' is a piece of all bearin', an' bearin' an' dyin' is two pieces of the same thing. An' then things ain't lonely any more. An' then a hurt don't hurt so bad, 'cause it ain't a lonely hurt no more, Rose-asharn. I wisht I could tell you so you'd know, but I can't."

Because Ma is so firm in her belief in the rightness of natural processes, she becomes furious at the religious hypocrites who plague the migrants. At the Hoovervilles and in the government station, the evangelists whom Ma characterizes as Holy Rollers and Jehovites are grimly present, like camp followers. Beginning with polite acceptance, Ma becomes infuriated when one of these zealots works on Rose of Sharon, scaring her half to death with visions of hellfire and burning. Ma represents the state of natural grace to which Casy aspires from the beginning.

Just as the novel reveals a preoccupation with biology, it is also obsessed with love of the earth. From the opening lines of the book, "To the red country and part of the gray country of Oklahoma, the last rains came gently, and they did not cut the scarred earth," to the last scene of desolation, the land imagery persists. The earth motif is woven into the texture complexly, but on the whole it serves two main functions: first, to signify love, and second, to signify endurance. Tom makes the sexual connection when, listening to Casy's compulsive story, he idly, but quite naturally, draws the torso of a woman in the dirt, "breasts, hips, pelvis." The attachment of the men to the land is often so intense that it borders on sexual love. Muley's refusal to leave, even after the caterpillar tractors have wiped him out, looks ahead to Grampa's similar recalcitrance. At first, Grampa is enthusiastic about the prospect of moving to a more fertile land, and he delivers himself of words verging on panegyric: "Jus' let me get out to California where I can pick me an orange when I want it. Or grapes. There's a thing I ain't ever had enough of. Gonna get me a whole big bunch of grapes off a bush, or whatever, an' I'm gonna squash 'em on my face, an' let 'em run offen my chin." But when the moment for departure arrives, Grampa refuses to go. His roots in the ground are too strong; he cannot bear to tear them up. Very soon after the family leaves its native soil, Grampa dies of a stroke. And when Casy says to Noah, "Grampa an' the old place, they was jus' the same thing," we feel that the observation has a precision which is supported by the texture of the entire novel. When the Joads get to California, they will, of course, find that the grapes which Grampa dreamed of are inaccessible, that the grapes of promise inevitably turn to grapes of wrath. The land, one interchapter tells, has been possessed by the men with a frantic hunger for land who came before the Joads. And the defeated promise is bitterly dramatized in the last scene, when a geranium, the last flower of earth to appear in the novel, becomes an issue dividing Ruthie and Winfield, and results in Ruthie's pressing one petal against Winfield's nose, cruelly. Love and endurance have been tried to their utmost. When the land goes, everything else goes, too; and the water is the emblem of its destruction.

Love of family parallels love of the earth. During the threatening instability of the cross-country journey, Ma Joad acts as the cohesive force which keeps her brood intact. Whenever one of the men threatens to leave, Ma protests, and sometimes savagely. When she takes over leadership of the family, by defying Pa Joad with a jack handle, it is over the question of whether or not Tom shall stay behind with the disabled car. Even after Connie, Rose of Sharon's husband, and Noah, one of the brothers, desert the family, the identity of the clan remains Ma Joad's primary fixation. After half a continent of hardship, Ma articulates her deepest feelings. She tells Tom, "They was a time when we was on the lan'. They was a boundary to us then. Ol' folks died off, an' little fellas came, an' we was always one thing—we was the fambly—kinda whole and clear. An' now we ain't clear no more." The deprivation of the native land, and the alienation of the new, become more than economic disasters; they threaten the only social organization upon which Ma Joad can depend. The fertility of the land and the integrity of the clan are no longer distinct entities; both are essential for survival.

Closely bound up with this theme of familial survival is the theme of human dignity. Clearly, the exigencies of eviction and migration force the problem of brute survival upon the Joads. But just as important is the correlative theme of human dignity. The first time the Joads are addressed as "Okies," by a loud-mouthed deputy who sports a Sam Browne belt and pistol holster, Ma is so shocked that she almost attacks him. Later, Uncle John is so chagrined by Casy's sacrificial act (deflecting from Tom the blame for hitting the deputy, and going to prison in his stead) that he feels positively sinful for not making an equal contribution. At the government camp, a woman complains about taking charity from the Salvation Army because "We was hungry—they made us crawl for our dinner. They took our dignity." But it is Tom who makes the most articulate defense of dignity against the legal harassment to which the Joads have been subjected: ". . . if it was the law they was workin' with, why, we could take it. But it *ain't* the law. They're a-workin' away at our spirits. . . . They're workin' on our decency." And the final image of Rose of Sharon offering her breast to the starving farmer is intended as an apotheosis of the scared girl, recently deprived of her child, into a kind of natural madonna.

In short, if the biological interest exists, it is so chastened through suffering that it achieves a dignity which is anything but animal, in Edmund Wilson's sense of the word. The conflicts, values, and recognitions of the Joads cannot, therefore, be equated with the preoccupations of subhuman life. The biological life may be retained in the search for food and shelter, in the cycle of death and procreation, but always in terms which emphasize rather than obliterate the distinctions between humans and animals. When Steinbeck reminisces in the *New York Times* (Sunday, November 27, 1955, Theatre Section, p. 1) about his carefree bohemian days in Monterey, he is just as nostalgic about the freedom of assorted drifters, his "interesting and improbable" characters, as he is about Ed Ricketts' "commercial biological laboratory." Steinbeck's novel may be read, then, as much as a flight from biological determinism as a representation of it. The story of the pilgrimage to the new Canaan which is California, the cycle of death and birth through which the Joads must suffer, becomes a moral, as well as a physical, trial by fire.

The socio-political implications of the Joad story, more familiar than these correlative themes, serve to counterpoint and define the anger and the suffering. Throughout the novel, the Joads are haunted by deputies in the service of landowners, bankers, and fruit growers; by the contradiction between endless acres in full harvest and streams of migratory workers in dire straits; by unscrupulous businessmen who take advantage of the desperate, westbound caravans; by strike-breakers, corrupt politicians, and thugs. At first, the Joads must draw from their meager savings to pay for gas and half-loaves of bread; but as they draw West they must even pay for water. In California, they cannot vote, are kept continually on the move, are bullied by the constabulary, and must even watch helplessly as one of the Hoovervilles is burned out. The only time they earn enough money to eat comes when they are hired as strike-breakers. Gradually, there is the dawning recognition that the only possible response to these impossible conditions is solidarity through union organization, precisely what the fruit growers and their agents dread most. In order to overcome the fruit growers' divisive tactics, Casy becomes an active union organizer and gets killed in the process by a bunch of marauding deputies. At the end, Tom, in his familiar farewell to Ma Joad, is trembling on the verge of Casy's solution. "That the end will be revolution," Earle Birney writes in *Canadian Forum* (June 1939, p. 95), "is implicit from the title onwards." Steinbeck ultimately withdraws from such a didactic conclusion, as we shall see in a moment, but that the didactic conclusion is implicit in the narrative can hardly be denied:

> . . . the companies, the banks worked at their own doom and they did not know it. The fields were fruitful, and starving men moved on the roads. The granaries were full and the children of the poor grew up rachitic, and the pustules of pellagra swelled on their sides. The great companies did not know that the line between hunger and anger is a thin line. And money that might have gone to wages went for gas, for guns, for agents and spies, for blacklists, for drilling. On the highways the people moved like ants and searched for work, for food. And the anger began to ferment.

Hence the symbolism of the title. Clearly woven through the novel, and therefore inseparable from Steinbeck's prose, we find these sharp political overtones. Besides being a novel, writes James N. Vaughan, *The Grapes of Wrath* "is a monograph on rural sociology, a manual of practical wisdom in times of enormous stress, an assault on individualism, an essay in behalf of a rather vague form of pantheism, and a bitter, ironical attack on that emotional evangelistic religion which seems to thrive in the more impoverished rural districts of this vast country." (*Commonweal*, July 28, 1949, pp. 341-42.)

Along the highways, a new social order is improvised, a fluid but permanent council in which the family is the basic unit, an order reaching its almost utopian operation at the government camp. According to this scheme, the governing laws remain constant, while the specific counters are continually replaced, one family succeeding another, a sort of permanent republic which can accommodate a populace in constant motion:

> The families learned what rights must be observed—the right of privacy in the tent; the right to keep the black past hidden in the heart; the right to talk and to listen; the right to refuse help or to decline it; the right of son to court and daughter to be courted; the right of the hungry to be fed; the rights of the pregnant and the sick to transcend all other rights. . . .
> And with the laws, the punishments—and there were only two—a quick and murderous fight or ostracism; and ostracism was the worst.

Within such a scheme, Ma Joad's fierce maintenance of the family becomes more clear. For without the integrity of the clan, survival is all but impossible. The alternatives are death, which does, in fact, snip the Joad family at both ends, claiming both the grandparents and Rose of Sharon's baby, or, on the other hand, militant struggle through union organization.

If the biological motifs do not appear in the film, these correlative themes are adopted with varying degrees of emphasis. The religious satire, with a single exception, is dropped entirely; the political radicalism is muted and generalized; but the insistence on family cohesion, on affinity for the land, on human dignity is carried over into the movie version.

In the film, the one remnant of tragi-comic religious satire occurs in Tom's first talk with Casy on the way to the Joad house. Casy's probing self-analysis is essentially the same as in the book, and its culmination, "There ain't no sin an' there ain't no virtue. There's just what people do," is a precise copy from the novel. Once the theme is enunciated, however, it is underplayed, recurring almost imperceptibly in the burial scene. Ma's anger at the evangelical camp followers is dropped entirely.

The film-makers must have known that the film was political dynamite. After a difficult decision, Darryl Zanuck began what turned out to be, thematically speaking, one of the boldest films in the history of the movies. The secrecy which surrounded the studios during production has become legend. Even as the film was being shot, Zanuck reportedly received fifteen thousand letters, ninety-nine per cent of which accused him of cowardice, saying he would never make the film because the industry was too closely associated with big business. And yet, as Frank Condon also reported in *Collier's* ("The Grapes of Raps," January 27, 1940), fearful that the Texas and Oklahoma Chambers of Commerce would object to the shooting on their territory of the *enfant terrible* of the publishing world, the studio announced that it was really filming another story innocuously entitled, *Highway 66*. It was precisely this fear of criticism, of giving offense to vested interests, that was responsible for muting the film's political implications. Lester Asheim has pointed out how the film scrupulously steers clear of the book's specific accusations. Many small episodes showing unfair business practices, for example, were cut from the film version. While the reference to the handbills which flood Oklahoma, luring an excess labor force out West, is carried over into the film, most of the corresponding details are dropped. The complaint about the unfair practices of used-car salesmen; the argument with the camp owner about overcharging; the depiction of the company-store credit racket; the dishonest scales on the fruit ranch; and even the practice, on the part of an otherwise sympathetic luncheon proprietor, of taking the jackpots from his own slot machines—none of these was ever even proposed for the shooting-script. Similarly, all legal authority is carefully exempt from blame. In Tom's angry speech about the indignities foisted upon the family by the local constabulary, everything is retained except his bitter indictment of the deputies, and his line, ". . . they comes a time when the on'y way a fella can keep his decency is by takin' a sock at a cop." In Casy's discourse on the progress of the fruit strike, the line, "An' all the cops in the worl' come down on us" is deleted. Casy's announcement that the cops have threatened to beat up recalcitrant strikers is retained, but the film adds, "Not them reg'lar deputies, but them tin badge fellas they call guards. . . ."

In spite of the revolutionary candor of the interchapters, whenever the film raises questions about whom to see or what to do for recourse or complaint, the novel's evasive answers are used in reply. When Tom asks the proprietor of the government camp why there aren't more places like this, the proprietor answers, "You'll have to find that out for yourself." When Muley wants to find out from the city man who's to blame for his eviction, so that he can take a shotgun to him, the city man tells him that the Shawnee Land and Cattle Company is so amorphous that it cannot be properly located. The bank in Tulsa is responsible for telling the land company what to do, but the bank's manager is simply an employee trying to keep up with orders from the East. "Then who do we shoot?" Muley asks in exasperation. "Brother, I don't know . . ." the city man answers helplessly. To add to the mystification, the film supplies a few clouds of its own. In the scene where Farmer Thomas warns Tom and the Wallaces about the impending raid on the government camp, the recurring question of "red" agitation comes up again. The "red menace" has become the *raison d'être* for attacks against the squatter camps. Tom, who has heard the argument before, bursts out, "What is these reds anyway?" Originally, according to the script, Wilkie Wallace was to have answered, cribbing his own line from the novel, that according to a fruit grower he knew once, a red is anyone who "wants thirty-cents an hour when I'm payin' twenty-five." In the final print, however, Farmer Thomas answers Tom's question simply but evasively, "I ain't talkin' about that one way 'r another," and goes on to warn the men about the raid.

Even Tom's much-quoted farewell to Ma Joad, retained in the film, is pruned until little remains but its mystical affirmation. And the final words, backing away from Casy's conscious social commitment, are carried over intact.

> MA: "I don' un'erstan. . . ."
> TOM: "Me neither, Ma. . . . It's jus' stuff I been thinkin' about. . . ."

In the world of the Ford-Johnson film, the politico-economic tendency is merely an urge in search of a name it is never allowed to find. And yet because of the naked suffering, the brute struggle to survive, devoid of solutions in either church or revolution, John Gassner in *Twenty Best Film Plays* finds that more appropriate than the image of God "trampling out the vintage where the grapes of wrath are stored," from which the title is derived, are the lines, "And here in dust and dirt . . . the lilies of his love appear," which connote neither religion nor politics. According to Gassner, bedrock is reached in this film, "and it proves to be as hard as granite and as soft as down."

If the religious satire is absent and the politics muted, the love of land, family, and human dignity are consistently translated into effective cinematic images. Behind the director's controlling hand is the documentary eye of a Pare Lorentz or a Robert Flaherty, of the vision in those stills produced by the Resettlement Administration in its volume, *Land of the Free* (with commentary by Archibald MacLeish), or in Walker Evans' shots for *Let Us Now Praise Famous Men* (with commentary by James Agee), which, like Lorentz's work, was carried on under the auspices of the Farm Security Administration. Gregg Toland's photography is acutely conscious of the pictorial values of land and sky, finding equivalents for those haunting images of erosion which were popularized for the New Deal's reclamation program and reflected in Steinbeck's prose. The constant use of brooding, dark silhouettes against light, translucent skies, the shots of roads and farms, the fidelity to the speech, manners, and dress of Oklahoma farmers —all contribute to the pictorial mood and tone. I was told in an interview with John Ford that some of these exteriors were shot on indoor sound stages at the studios, but even this has worked to the advantage of the film-makers. In the studio, Ford was able to control his composition by precise lighting, so that some of the visuals—Tom moving like an ant against a sky bright with luminous clouds, the caravans of jalopies, the slow rise of the dust storm—combine physical reality with careful composition to create striking pictorial effects. Finally, generous selections of dialogue, culled from the novel, echoing the theme of family affiliation with the land, appear in the final movie version. Grampa's last minute refusal to go, as he clutches at a handful of soil, necessitates Tom's plan to get him drunk and carry him aboard by force. And, as Muley, John Qualen's apostrophe to the land, after the tractor has plowed into his shack, is one of the most poignant anywhere in films.

In the same fashion, the central episodes depicting Ma Joad's insistence on family cohesion, and Tom's insistence on dignity, are either presented directly or clearly suggested. Ma, to be sure, is made a little less fierce than she is in the novel. Tom still tells Casy the anecdote about Ma's taking after a tin peddler with an ax in one hand and a chicken in the other, but the scene in which she takes a jack handle after Pa, originally scheduled according to the script, is deleted. We never see Ma physically violent.

Tracing through these recurring themes, comparing and contrasting the emphasis given to each, gives us all the advantages of content analysis without explaining, finally, the central difference between Steinbeck's artistic vision and that of the film-makers. This difference does emerge, however, when we compare the two structures.

Some deletions, additions, and alterations, to be sure, reflect in a general way the ordinary process of mutation from a linguistic to a visual medium. On the one hand, the characteristic interchapters in the novel are dropped entirely, those interludes which adopt the author's point of view and which are at once more lyric and less realistic than the rest of the prose. The angry interludes, the explicit indictments, the authorial commentary do not appear, indeed would seem obtrusive, in the film. Translated into observed reality, however, and integrated into the picture within the frame, certain fragments find their proper filmic equivalents. For example, the interchapters are mined for significant dialogue, and, in fact, Muley's moving lines, "We were born on it, and we got killed on it, died on it. Even if it's no good, it's still ours. . . ." appear originally in one of these interludes. In the second place, the themes of one or two of these interchapters are translated into a few highly effective montages—the coming of the tractors, the caravans of jalopies, the highway signs along Route 66. As Muley begins telling his story, over the candle in the dimly lit cabin, the film flashes back to the actual scene. A series of tractors looming up like mechanical creatures over the horizon, crossing and crisscrossing the furrowed land, cuts to the one tractor driven by the Davis boy, who has been assigned the task of clearing off Muley's farm. Later, as the Joads' jalopy begins its pilgrimage, we see a similar shot of scores and scores of other jalopies, superimposed one upon the other, making the same, slow, desperate cross-country trek. Finally, the central episodes of the trip are bridged by montages of road signs—"Checotah, Oklahoma City, Bethany," and so on to California. These devices have the effect of generalizing the conflicts of the Joads, of making them representative of typical problems in a much wider social context. In every reversal, in every act of oppression, we feel the pressure of thousands.

If the film carries these striking equivalents of Steinbeck's prose, it is due partly to the assistance which Steinbeck offers the film-maker, partly to the visual imagination of the film-maker himself. Except for the freewheeling omniscience of the interchapters, the novel's prose relies wholly on dialogue and physical action to reveal character. Because Steinbeck's style is not marked by meditation, it resembles, in this respect, the classic form of the scenario. Even at moments of highest tension, Steinbeck scrupulously avoids getting inside the minds of his people. Here is Ma right after Tom has left her, and probably forever:

> "Good-by" she said, and she walked quickly away. . . . Her footsteps were loud and careless on the leaves as she went through the brush. And as she went, out of the dim sky the rain began to fall, big drops and few, splashing on the dry leaves heavily. Ma stopped and stood still in the dripping thicket. She turned about—took three steps back toward the mound of vines; and then she turned quickly and went back toward the boxcar camp.

Although this is Steinbeck's characteristic style, it can also serve as precise directions for the actor. There is nothing here which cannot be turned into images of physical reality. Critics who seem surprised at the ease with which Steinbeck's work moves from one medium to another may find their explanation here. Precisely this fidelity to physical detail was responsible, for example, for the success of *Of Mice and Men* first as a novel, then as a play, then as a film. And yet, in *The Grapes of Wrath,* the film-makers rethought the material for themselves, and frequently found more exact cinematic keys to the mood and color of particular scenes in the book. Often their additions are most effective in areas where the novel is powerless—in moments of silence. Casy jumping over a fence and tripping, after the boast about his former preaching prowess; Ma Joad burning her keepsakes (the little dog from the St. Louis Exposition, the old letters, the card from Pa); the earrings which she saves, holding them to her ears in the cracked mirror, while the sound track carries the muted theme from "Red River Valley"; the handkerchiefs which Tom and Casy hold to their mouths in the gathering dust; Tom laboriously adding an "s" to "funerl" in the note which will accompany Grampa to his grave; the reflection of Al, Tom, and Pa in the jalopy's windshield at night as the family moves through the hot, eerie desert—all these, while they have no precedent in the novel, make for extraordinarily effective cinema. The images are clean and precise, the filmic signature of a consistent collaboration between John Ford and his cameraman.

The deletions, on one level, are sacrifices to the exigencies of time and plot. The dialogue is severely pruned. Most of the anecdotes are dropped, along with the curse words. And the leisurely, discursive pace of the novel gives way to a tightly knit sequence of events. The episodes involving the traveling companionship of the Wilsons, the desertions of Noah and Connie; the repeated warnings about the dismal conditions in California from bitterly disappointed migrants who are traveling home the other way; and countless other small events do not appear in the film story, though a few of them, such as Noah's desertion, appeared in the script and were even shot during production. But the moment we go from an enumeration of these deletions to the arrangement of sequences in the final work, we have come to our central structural problem.

As I indicated earlier, the structure of the book resembles a parabola in which the high point is the successful thwarting of the riot at the government camp. Beginning with Tom's desolate return to his abandoned home, the narrative proceeds through the journey from Oklahoma to California; the Hooverville episodes; the government-camp episodes; the strike-breaking episodes at the Hooper Ranch; Tom's departure; the flooding of the cotton pickers' boxcar camp; the last scene in the abandoned farm. From the privation and dislocation of the earlier episodes, the Joads are continually plagued, threatened with dissolution, until, through the gradual knitting of strength and resistance, the family finds an identity which coincides with its experience at the government camp. Here they are startled by the sudden absence of everything from which they have been running—dirty living conditions, external compulsion, grubbing for survival, brutal policemen, unscrupulous merchants. They find, instead, a kind of miniature planned economy, efficiently run, boasting modern sanitation, self-government, co-operative living, and moderate prices. After their departure from the camp, the fortunes of the Joads progressively deteriorate, until that desolate ending which depicts Rose of Sharon's still-born child floating downstream.* The critical response to Steinbeck's shocking ending was almost universally negative. Clifton Fadiman in *The New Yorker* called it the "tawdriest kind of fake symbolism." Anthony West in *The New Statesman and Nation* attributed it to the novel's "astonishingly awkward" form. Louis Kronenberger in the *Nation* found that the entire second half of the book "lacks form and intensity . . . ceases to grow, to maintain direction," but did not locate the reasons for his dissatisfaction. Malcolm Cowley, in spite of general enthusiasm, found in *The New Republic* the second half less impressive than the first because Steinbeck "wants to argue as if he weren't quite sure of himself." Charles Angoff in the *North American Review* was one of a small minority who defended both the ending and the "robust looseness" of the novel as squarely in the narrative tradition of Melville, Cervantes, and Thomas Hardy.

Contrast these objections with the general approval of the film's structure. Thomas Burton in the *Saturday Review of Literature* becomes adulatory over Ford's "incessant physical intimacy and fluency." Otis Ferguson in *The New Republic* speaks in superlatives: "This is a best that has no very near

---

* The scene usually denounced by critics is that at the end of Chapter Thirty in which Rose of Sharon offers her breast to a starving old man.—ED.

comparison to date. . . . It all moves with the simplicity and perfection of a wheel across silk." Why did the film-makers merit such a sharply contrasting critical reception? Simply because they corrected the objectionable structure of the novel. First, they deleted the final sequence; and second, they accomplished one of the most remarkable narrative switches in film history. Instead of ending with the strike-breaking episodes in which Tom is clubbed, Casy killed, and the strikers routed, the film ends with the government-camp interlude. This reversal, effected with almost surgical simplicity, accomplishes, in its metamorphic power, an entirely new structure which has far-reaching consequences. Combined with the deletion of the last dismal episode, and the pruning, alterations, and selections we have already traced, the new order changes the parabolic structure to a straight line that continually ascends. Beginning with the desolate scene of the dust storm, the weather in the film improves steadily with the fortunes of the Joads, until, at the end, the jalopy leaves the government camp in sunlight and exuberant triumph. Even a sign, called for in the original script, which might have darkened the rosy optimism that surrounds the departing buggy, does not appear in the cut version. The sign was to have read, "No Help Wanted." As in the novel, Tom's departure is delayed until the end, but the new sequence of events endows his farewell speech with much more positive overtones. In place of the original ending, we find a line that appears [near] the end of Chapter Twenty, exactly two-thirds of the way through the book. It is Ma's strong assurance, "We'll go on forever, Pa. We're the people." On a thematic level, as Asheim points out, the affirmative ending implies that action is not required since the victims of the situation will automatically emerge triumphant. "Thus the book, which is an exhortation to action, becomes a film which offers reassurance that no action is required to insure the desired resolution of the issue." But the film's conclusion has the advantage of seeming structurally more acceptable. Its "new logic" affords a continuous movement which, like a projectile, carries everything before it. The movie solution satisfies expectations which are there in the novel to begin with and which the novel's ending does not satisfactorily fulfill. Hence the critics' conflicting reaction to the two endings. Where the book seems to stop and meander in California, the film displays a forward propulsion that carries well on beyond the Colorado River.

Is such an inversion justified? Nunnally Johnson reports that he chose Ma's speech for his curtain line because he considered it the "real" spirit of Steinbeck's book. This might seem at first like brazen tampering. But Johnson further reports that from Steinbeck himself he receivd *carte blanche* to make any alterations he wished. Steinbeck defended his position on the grounds that a novelist's final statement is in his book. Since the novelist can add nothing more, the film-maker is obliged to remake the work in his own style. If Steinbeck's awareness of the adaptational process is not enough, we may also find internal justification for the film-maker's brilliantly simple reversal. We have seen how the production crew effected alternations which mute the villainy of cops and tradesmen; underplay the religious satire; cloud over the novel's political radicalism. But part of this withdrawal has precedent in the novel itself. The city man's portrayal of the anonymity of the banks; the proprietor's evasive answer to Tom in the government camp; Ma and Tom's mystical faith—these are all Steinbeck's. So is the fact that from the beginning Tom is on parole, which he technically breaks by leaving the state. Already he is outside the domain of legal ordinance. Tom is a fugitive who *has* to keep running. If the film's conclusion withdraws from a leftist commitment, it is because the novel does also. If the film vaporizes radical sociology, the novel withdraws from it, too, with Rose of Sharon's final act. The familial optimism of the one and the biological pessimism of the other are two sides of the same coin.

The structural achievement of the cinematic version may account, paradoxically, for the film's troubling reputation. On the one hand, acclamation, box-office success, critical enthusiasm; Jane Darwell winning an Academy Award for her portrayal of Ma Joad; the casting and acting of Henry Fonda, John Carradine, Charley Grapewin, Al Qualen, Frank Darien, Grant Mitchell, and the others, generally considered flawless; Nunnally Johnson sporting a gold plaque on the wall of his studio office in recognition of a fine screenplay; and one reporter (Michel Mok in the *Nation*, February 3, 1940, pp. 127-28) poking fun at the grandiose première of the film at the Normandie Theatre in New York, which was attended by glamorous stars adorned in jewels and furs, and, like a "Blue Book pilgrimage," by the representatives of the very banks and land companies that had tractored the Joads off their farms. Zanuck and his entourage must have known that the filmic portrait of Steinbeck's book was no serious threat.

On the other hand, the industry's discomfort. *The Grapes of Wrath* came as close as any film in Hollywood's prolific turn-out to exposing the contradictions and inequities at the heart of American life. A new thing had been created and its implications were frightening. In spite of its facile conclusion, the film raises questions to which others, outside the fictive world, have had to supply answers. The film's unusual cinematographic accomplishments, its structural unity, its documentary realism, combine to fashion images, embodying those questions, which one may review with profit again and again. If the novel is remembered for its moral anger, the film is remembered for its beauty. And yet the industry has been a little embarrassed by its success. That success and that embarrassment may help explain why Nunnally Johnson has accomplished so little of lasting interest since his work on this film, and why he was last seen completing the scenario for Sloan Wilson's *The Man in the Gray Flannel Suit*, a book of a very different kind! It may explain why John Ford never lists *The Grapes* as one of his favorite films, and why Ford himself offers perhaps the best explanation for the film's unique personality. Tersely, but with just the slightest trace of whimsy and bravado, John Ford remarks, "I never read the book."

THE CAST OF *The Grapes of Wrath*
THE JOAD PARTY

Grampa	*Charley Grapewin*
Granma	*Zeffie Tilbury*
Pa	*Russell Simpson*
Ma	*Jane Darwell*
Noah	*Frank Sully*
Tom	*Henry Fonda*
Rosasharn	*Doris Bowdon*
Connie Rivers	*Eddie Quillan*
Al	*O. Z. Whitehead*
Ruthie	*Shirley Mills*
Winfield	*Darryl Hickman*
Uncle John	*Frank Darien*
Casy	*John Carradine*

Al Qualen played Muley Graves, and Ward Bond and Grant Mitchell appeared in supporting roles.

CHAPTER 9

Is The Grapes of Wrath
Art or Propaganda?

WHEN GEORGE BLUESTONE OBSERVES THAT STEINBECK'S novel is remembered for its "moral anger," whereas the film version is remembered for its "beauty," he touches upon the longest lasting controversy provoked by *The Grapes of Wrath.* In less than a quarter of a century, critical reaction to the novel has passed through three phases. Although the fashionable terms of dispute vary, the two viewpoints involved remain constant. The quarrel stems basically from the long hostility between those two factions in American culture that Philip Rahv in *Image and Idea* (1949) calls "Redskins" and "Palefaces."

The "Palefaces," maintaining the genteel tradition of the Boston brahmins, hold that literature should concern itself only with cultured people, not with Whitman's beloved "roughs"; whereas the "Redskins" revel, like Whitman— "I will not have a single person slighted or left away"—in depicting the full range of American society. "Palefaces" are also convinced that no work that becomes a best-seller can be art. *The Grapes of Wrath* is thus doubly suspect: because of Steinbeck's concern with riff-raff and because of the novel's sales record. Reluctant to avow their snobbery openly, the "Palefaces" have devised various stratagems by which to rationalize their prejudices; writers whose subject matter they find distasteful are often charged with sentimentality, or with treating people like animals.

The artistic merits of Steinbeck's novel have, of course, been stanchly defended. Perhaps the greatest literary tribute paid it is the concluding statement in Alexander Cowie's *The Rise of the American Novel* (1949) that "in Steinbeck's *The Grapes of Wrath* most of the new features [in American fiction] that have any value find a brilliant and powerful synthesis."

Not all literary historians have concurred in this generous verdict. At first, scholarly critics regarded the novel as simply propaganda, rather than art. In *The Novels of John Steinbeck* (1939), a study which appeared shortly after *The Grapes of Wrath*, Harry T. Moore said that the novel's main story "never comes to life the way it should." Joseph Warren Beach in *American Fiction 1920-1940* (1942) compared the appeal of the novel to that of *Robinson Crusoe*, but qualified his enthusiasm by saying that *The Grapes of Wrath* is "perhaps the finest example we have so far produced in the United States of the proletarian novel," which he defined loosely as dealing with "any social or industrial problem from the point of view of labor." Alfred Kazin in *On Native Grounds* (1942) described Steinbeck's book as "the most influential social novel of its period," "as urgent and as obvious a social tract for its time as *Uncle Tom's Cabin* had been for another." He went on to say, however, that the novel gave Americans "a design, a sense of control, where out of other depression novels they could get only the aimless bombardment of rage." Maxwell Geismar observed in *Writers in Crisis* (1941) that *The Grapes of Wrath* "often represents the dubious nuptials of 'Tobacco

Road' with the *Ladies' Home Journal*," but added that the "force and sincerity" of the novel allow it to "break through the moulds of its presentation." Trying to balance the claims of "Paleface" and "Redskin," Geismar judged that since *The Grapes of Wrath* has "the same urgency which in Zola's [*Germinal*] holds us some fifty years after its inception, . . . it will be condemned only by those who, in the end, prefer perfection to importance."

Some perfection seekers were not appeased. One of the most distinguished "Palefaces," Edmund Wilson, in *The Boys in the Back Room* (1941) wrote what remains the most sweeping condemnation of the novel. Wilson found the Okies "not quite real," because "in spite of Mr. Steinbeck's attempts to make them figure as heroic human symbols, one cannot help feeling that they, too, do not quite exist seriously for him as people. It is as if human sentiments and speeches had been assigned to a flock of lemmings on their way to throw themselves into the sea." Wilson's influential judgment was challenged very early by one of the most persuasive proponents of the "Redskin" viewpoint, Frederic I. Carpenter, in an essay entitled "The Philosophical Joads" (1941). The ideas Steinbeck voices through his character Jim Casy, said Carpenter, "continue, develop, integrate, and realize the thought of the great writers of American history. Here the mystical transcendentalism of Emerson reappears, and the earthy democracy of Whitman, and the pragmatic instrumentalism of William James and John Dewey. . . . The enduring greatness of *The Grapes of Wrath* consists in its imaginative realization of these old ideas in new and concrete forms."

The first phase of the criticism of the novel ended as American participation in World War II resolved the specific, local problem around which the novel had developed. As B. R. McElderry, Jr., pointed out in *"The Grapes of Wrath:* In the Light of Modern Critical Theory" (1944), conditions had changed as greatly in five years as they normally do in a generation. The novel had outlived its purely propagandistic function; and, if it was to survive, it must do so on its artistic merits. By testing the novel against some of the doctrines of the then rising New Criticism, and those doctrines against the novel, McElderry succeeded in presenting as objective an evaluation of *The Grapes of Wrath* as any of its early critics; his essay is reprinted in the following pages as an assessment of the stature of the work at a time when a sensational novel of only transient interest would have begun to sink into oblivion.

After World War II, long-silenced voices from abroad—including that of the Existentialist philosopher Jean-Paul Sartre, whose article in the *Atlantic Monthly* has been quoted on page 150, began to make Americans realize that *The Grapes of Wrath* could no longer be regarded as merely a tract. Some American critics, however, retreating from the position that the novel was simply propaganda, rephrased their attacks and now maintained that it was a specimen not of art, but of artfulness—that its author had simply sought, despite his explicit disclaimer, to "cash in" on the misery of the migrants. This attitude colors the treatment of the novel in the two postwar histories of American literature.

In *The Literary History of the United States* (1948), Maxwell Geismar, whose earlier opinion is quoted above, now spoke of *The Grapes of Wrath*, "recalling as it did the historical meaning of the frontier in terms of social crisis," as "a big and life-giving book," but observed that "an emotional facility and simplification of experience . . . kept Steinbeck's whole achievement from being as impressive as it was arresting." George F. Whicher in *The Literature of the American People* (1951) wrote more bluntly: "There is brilliant writing in *The Grapes of Wrath*'s memorable descriptions, episodes of moving power, forceful exposition of social injustice. Yet on reflection the final impression left by the novel is not of the author's indignation so much as of his cleverness as a contriver of effects." Frederick Hoffman, writing in *The Modern Novel in America* also in 1951, had doubts even about the cleverness, commenting that "the worst strategy of all, the philosophical, involves what are perhaps some of the most wretched violations of aesthetic taste observable in modern American fiction," while Edward Wagenknecht in *Cavalcade of the American Novel* (1952) found that the novel has "no real climax or termination" and that the novelist sometimes "analyzes where he ought to portray."

Curiously, although the controversy over the merits and classification of Steinbeck's novel has long persisted, the issue of its artfulness versus its art has been fully debated in print only once. In 1954 Bernard Bowron, a member of the American Studies faculty at the University of Minnesota, contributed to *The Colorado Quarterly* an essay maintaining that the success of Steinbeck's novel rested upon his artful exploitation of the conventions of the stereotyped "covered wagon" romance. The editor of this *Companion* challenged Bowron's thesis, in a later issue of the same magazine, and defended both the originality and artistic structure of *The Grapes of Wrath*. Both papers are reprinted here, as the clearest confrontation among published discussions of the novel of the viewpoints of the "Paleface," preoccupied with literary models, and the "Redskin," obsessed with the realities of the American experience.

Not long after this debate—to which John Steinbeck himself contributed a brief afternote, declining to take sides and describing new critical writing in general as "an ill tempered parlor game in which nobody gets kissed"—*The Grapes of Wrath* began to receive more intensive and more respectful treatment than critics had previously given it. E. W. Tedlock, Jr., and C. V. Wicker's anthology *Steinbeck and His Critics* (1957) and Peter Lisca's book-length study of the author and his work, *The Wide World of John Steinbeck* (1958), made available a variety of thoughtful and detailed analyses. Robert Spiller noted in *The Cycle of American Literature* (1955) that the novel remains, after the controversy over its tractarian character has died down, "an American epic, a culminating expression of the spiritual and material forces that had discovered and settled a continent."

Spiller is premature, however, in his assumption that the controversy is over, for in 1959 R. W. B. Lewis could write in an article called "Fitful Daemon" (in *The Young Rebel in American Literature*, edited by Carl Bode) that "*The Grapes of Wrath* does not manage to transcend its political theme because the question 'What is man?' was not really accepted by Steinbeck as the root question." Lewis goes on to say, "The application of Steinbeck's special and happy-natured poetry to his newly discovered and unhappy historical materials could only result in a defeat of the poetry." Lewis's unfavorable assessment exemplifies a recent tendency to treat *The Grapes of Wrath* not as a conventional novel but as a kind of prose epic, displaying qualities principally associated with poetry. This tendency is evidenced also in Maxwell Geismar's third judgment of the novel—which balances Lewis's—in *A Time of Harvest* (1962). Geismar writes that this "key work of its period" is "in some respects an epic chronicle of the depression years in our western agrarian culture."

With its epic qualities, *The Grapes of Wrath* has also been found to contain Biblical parallels, which were pointed out as early as 1939 by Harry T. Moore, and have been studied extensively since the appearance in 1956 of Martin S. Shockley's essay, "Christian Symbolism in *The Grapes of Wrath*." These parallels are summed up in H. Kelly Crockett's "The Bible and *The Grapes of Wrath*," as well as in two less comprehensive discussions: Gerard Cannon's "The Pauline Apostleship of Tom Joad" and Charles T. Dougherty's "The Christ-Figure in *The Grapes of Wrath*," all published in *College English*, December 1962. Thomas F. Dunn comments upon and suggests additions to Crockett's remarks in a "Rebuttal" in *College English*, April 1963. The most impressive recent discussion of the novel is J. Paul Hunter's contribution to a collection, *Essays in Modern American Literature* (1963), which defends the novel once again as art rather than "sociology," and traces in impressive detail not only the Biblical imagery but also the theme of conversion that runs through it.

Hunter concludes his essay with a statement about the final scene that sums up briefly but cogently what sensitive critics have discovered from close readings of the novel:

As the Joads hover in the one dry place in their world —a barn—the Bible's three major symbols of a purified order are suggested: the Old Testament deluge, the New Testament stable, and the continuing ritual of communion. In the fusion of the three, the novel's mythic background, ideological progression, and modern setting are brought together: Mount Ararat, Bethlehem, and California are collapsed into a single unit of time, and life is affirmed in a massive symbol of regeneration.

As this suggests, *The Grapes of Wrath*, properly understood, might go far toward healing the split Philip Rahv finds in the personality of our national literature. Hunter shows that the writer about the lowlife world of the "Redskin" may adroitly use the favorite medium of the "Paleface"—allegory—to reaffirm the enduring values of the very cultural heritage cherished by 'refined' society.

As Hunter's attention to the last scene of the novel indicates, the continuing quarrel over *The Grapes of Wrath* has tended to focus not so much upon the interpretation of the whole narrative as upon the final tableau in which Rose of Sharon Joad, whose baby has been stillborn, offers her milk to a starving old man whom the remaining members of the Joad family find in the barn where they seek refuge from a storm. Ever since Clifton Fadiman observed in *The New Yorker* that this ending was the "tawdriest kind of fake symbolism," critics offended by its uncompromising realism have denounced this poignant scene. Even in the standard reference work *The Oxford Companion to American Literature*, James D. Hart speaks, in a biographical sketch of Steinbeck, of the author's "failure to complete the story of *The Grapes of Wrath*, the value of whose conclusion is purely symbolic."

As I have pointed out in my own *John Steinbeck*, "the tableau does not halt an unfinished story," but "marks the end of the story Steinbeck had to tell about the Joads," whose "education is completed." Few attempts have been made, however, to clarify the synthesis of realistic and symbolic elements in this singularly appropriate concluding scene. Theodore Pollock's "On the Ending of *The Grapes of Wrath*" is therefore reprinted as the concluding selection in this *Companion* because of the evidence it affords that *The Grapes of Wrath* offers hitherto unperceived rewards to the sensitive and sympathetic reader.

B. R. McElderry, Jr.
The Grapes of Wrath: *In the Light of Modern Critical Theory*

The social problem which made the Joads of national significance in 1939 has disappeared or changed its form. The artistic problem of their chronicle remains. Now, as in 1939, the devil asks the conundrum of the workshop: "It's clever, but is it *art?*" To literary students the question is important, for it seems likely that in the generation to come we shall have more rather than less of propaganda literature. And, since events of the last five years have altered our perspective as much as might ordinarily be expected in a generation, it is worth while just now to reconsider the ablest production of one of our ablest novelists.

The attempt is the more timely, because of the present emphasis on critical values and methods. In discussing *The Grapes of Wrath*, I am going to use a number of ideas found in two books of critical theory published by the Princeton University Press; they are *The Intent of the Critic* [Donald A. Stauffer, editor] and *The Intent of the Artist* [Augusto Centeno, editor]. (The distinction of the titles is unimportant, for even an artist turns critic when he talks about his art.) Each of these books is in form a symposium, with no great unity of plan.

From *College English*, V (March 1944), 308-313. Reprinted by permission of the author and of the National Council of Teachers of English.

Though not intended to be a consistent body of doctrine, these books do bring together conveniently a number of ideas actually operative in the making and reading of contemporary literature. If, then, we take these ideas, we have a tangible basis for evaluating the novel; and, conversely, we have our experience with the novel as a check upon the theories.

First, let us consider the old question of the basic relationship of art and reality, a point most fully discussed by Mr. Centeno in his Introduction to *The Intent of the Artist.* He asserts that there are two theories of art: art is an irreducible activity, a love activity complete within itself and justified by its own existence; or art is merely a pleasanter way of representing materials found in purer form elsewhere. Of these two theories, Mr. Centeno prefers the first; in fact, he denies the validity of the second. According to which theory, then, was *The Grapes of Wrath* written? Or does either theory sufficiently account for the novel?

It is certainly true that Steinbeck does seem in a sense to be in love with his characters and with the living tissue of their experience. One thinks of Tom Joad going home from prison, of his welcome when he finds his family the next morning, of Granpa's funeral at the roadside. Such scenes do illustrate Mr. Centeno's observation that an artist is "a man who cannot separate himself from livingness." Parenthetically, I may remark that I do not consider "livingness" a term of great beauty; but as a paraphrase for "vividness," it at least avoids the hackneyed, smooth-worn quality of that overused term.

Yet in spite of the "livingness," or the love of life, embodied in Steinbeck's depiction of scene and character, it is true that parts of the novel—the rage against the bankers of Oklahoma, the camp life of the Okies in California, the fruit-ranch strike— may fairly be described as a "pleasanter" representation of facts to be found in purer form elsewhere. Carey McWilliams' *Factories in the Field,* a contemporary work of popular economics and sociology, affords convenient comparison. In factual truth

McWilliams' work is fuller and more authentic; though at the same time Steinbeck's novel is more lively, or, to use Mr. Centeno's angular term, more full of "livingness." The novel might thus be said to illustrate both the theories of art described by Mr. Centeno. Yet Mr. Centeno has presented these two theories as mutually exclusive; in so far as the novel competes with *Factories in the Field,* he would say, it is false and unsatisfactory as a work of art.

Further on in his discussion, however, we find Mr. Centeno asserting that "the work of art is not meant to be a corroboration of our sense of experience, but an expansion of it." Now, obviously, the sense of experience must be corroborated before it can be expanded. In *The Grapes of Wrath,* for instance, the foreclosures of Oklahoma, the camp life of California, and the fruit-ranch strike must be made plausible before their effects on the characters becomes of interest. Thus Mr. Centeno's original statement of the two theories as opposed and mutually exclusive seems misleading. It illustrates, I believe, the favorite academic sin of thinking in categories instead of in dynamics. If *The Grapes of Wrath* is a bad novel, it cannot reasonably be condemned on the grounds that it is sociological. It would be impossible to write a novel on the Okies that would not be sociological. It is possible, however, that the sociology might be inartistically presented or that the sociology might be bad to begin with.

Before proceeding further with this basic issue, let us consider the related point of unity—an old requirement for a work of art. To the familiar idea of the vital relationship between author, subject, and reader, Mr. Centeno introduces a new subtlety of terminology. Thus the intent of the artist is distinguished from his intentions. His intentions are conscious, willed purposes; while the intent, subconscious and innate, is represented as more deeply vital, and hence especially characteristic of the masterpiece.

In terms of *The Grapes of Wrath,* I take this distinction to mean something like this. Steinbeck's intention was to write a story of the Joad family in its struggle to adapt itself to new, unfavorable conditions. In carrying out this conscious intention and in writing the various scenes which represent subintentions, Steinbeck's real interest—his subconscious motivation—is to express his basic faith in mankind, in the courage, the endurance, and the kindliness of people like the Joads, and to show their passionate yearning for opportunity and for justice. It is the presence of this intent which gives power to the intention —that is, if one concedes that the novel is successful.

The content of the work of art, says Mr. Centeno, must be formally organized in accordance with the creative intent. Thus, in *The Grapes of Wrath* the first quarter of the volume concerns preparations for the trip west; the second quarter, the trip itself, and the latter half, the sequence leading to Tom's escape, Al's engagement, and the birth of Rosasharn's baby. This cycle of events, I believe, is adequate to embody the intent: Steinbeck's feeling for the fundamental nature of his characters.

The relation of the work of art to the reader or audience is termed by Mr. Centeno its "extent." In securing extent—or perhaps one might substitute the common phrase "reader-interest" —the intent must not be sacrificed or impaired. In *The Grapes of Wrath*, for example, it might be a question as to whether the freedom of language is always essential to the intent, or whether a few "sons-of-bitches" are sometimes thrown in to increase the extent of the book among certain readers. More seriously, some passages might be considered as direct propaganda and hence a distraction from the basic intent. My own conclusion, based on a fourth reading of the novel, is that it does have "integral creative oneness," in Mr. Centeno's exact but cumbersome phrase. The intent seems to me clear and steady; the content well selected, arranged, and proportioned; and the extent, or communication of intent to the reader, is adequate. One notable exception is the concluding detail in which Rosasharn gives her breast to the starving stranger. This incident,

clearly symbolic of the basic intent, is, nevertheless, not sufficiently plausible to communicate it. Coming at the very end of
the novel, the incident is an important exception. This, and perhaps a few other details aside, however, the novel remains
"interesting," not "exteresting," in Mr. Centeno's use of these
terms. In the historical sense any novel about the Okies would
be "exteresting" if it contained something of factual or sociological truth. But a novel on this subject would be interesting
only if it were felt integrally—that is, if it had inner unity. Such
an inner unity I believe *The Grapes of Wrath* has.

Turning to *The Intent of the Critic,* we find in Mr. [John
Crowe] Ransom's discussion of poetry two ideas which may,
I think, be adapted to the discussion of the novel. First, says
Mr. Ransom, "a poem is more than its paraphrase." Now, in
the loose sense of the term, anything printed or spoken is more
than its paraphrase; but the implication of Mr. Ransom's
statement is that a poem must, in the actual line-for-line reading of it, create itself. The means by which it does this, he says,
are its structure and texture; these, then, are the proper—or
most important—considerations for the critic.

That structure is as valuable to a novel as it is to a poem is
well illustrated by *The Grapes of Wrath.* Yet it has not been
sufficiently recognized, I think, that *The Grapes of Wrath*—
like the *Odyssey, Pilgrim's Progress,* and *Robinson Crusoe*—
is formulated as a journey. This structural device—one of the
simplest, oldest, and most vital in literature—is well suited to
the theme or intent of the story: the search for opportunity and
justice. This, I believe, will be generally admitted. The ending
of the story, however (not the Rosasharn incident previously
mentioned, but the final disposition of the characters), has been
severely criticized. I remember a friend of mine saying, "It
doesn't *have* any ending." This, he felt, was a defect in the
novel which clearly revealed the author's incompetence. But the
lack of an ending in any final sense is in keeping with the basic
idea of the novel. The continued faith in the search, in spite of

failure to find opportunity and justice, is far more effective than a trumped-up ending (such as the conclusion to *Robinson Crusoe*) would be. In a way, the uncompleted journey toward opportunity and justice is parallel to the modern tragedy, which decrees life, not death, for its hero.

Of the texture of a novel it is difficult to speak without long extracts. Several points, however, may be indicated briefly. There is the dialogue, with its rich, illiterate idiom; the description—set pieces, like the turtle crossing the road, and details which help us realize such a scene as the government camp; narrative episodes, such as the desert ride; and dramatic scenes, such as the burning of Hooverville. One may say that the texture is varied; that the pace is swift; that the story is fully rather than barely told. And one may say that the temptation to skip —even in re-reading—seldom appears.

A special problem is presented by the notable interludes, which treat the background of the Joads' experience: the opening chapter, descriptive of the dust bowl; the sale of household goods and the purchase of secondhand cars, set forth in a strangely generalized but vivid dialogue; the decay of the vacant houses; and the chaos of U.S. Highway 66. Of the thirty chapters in the novel, fourteen are interludes of this sort, though they occupy less than a hundred of its six hundred pages. They are Steinbeck's chief departure from conventional technique, and obviously they are a departure only in degree. Novelists have always felt free to elaborate the physical and social setting of the story. Steinbeck's interludes enrich the texture of his novel, and they do it far more subtly than, say, the moral essays of Fielding; or the "Dear Reader" passages of Dickens and Thackeray; or, to come closer to date, the elaborate author-interpretation of Galsworthy. To change the basis of comparison, the interludes have much the same justification and effectiveness as the familiar "long shots" of the movies. Of the fourteen interludes, only five are bare and direct social criticism voiced by the author rather than his characters. These are the conception of the soulless banks and corporations in Chapter Five; the concept of Manself as opposed to ownership in Chapter Fourteen; the history of landownership in California; the Californian suspicion of the Okies; and the indictment of waste under the profit system. In defense of these passages it may be said that they comprise barely twenty-five pages of the six-hundred-page novel; that they are so spaced as to bear upon the story itself (for example, the history of landownership in California comes just before the Joads enter Hooverville); that their illiterate eloquence points up the colloquial tone of the book as a whole. Leave these passages out, and something valuable, something pertinent, is gone.

Approval of the novel on the basis of its structure and texture, however, would not satisfy Mr. Norman Foerster, whose essay [in *The Intent of the Critic*] sets up ethical considerations as equally important with aesthetic ones. It is, he says, the business of the artist to achieve aesthetic and ethical values together, in whatever way he can; it is the business of the critic to distinguish between these values. From poetry he gives two brief examples of such discrimination. Of Wordsworth's "Tintern Abbey" he says that it "is great aesthetically; as we have come increasingly to see, it is ethically vital, but unsound; in sum, this poem is a superb expression of unwisdom." And of Longfellow's "Psalm of Life" Mr. Foerster remarks that it is "bungling in its art, stereotyped in its wisdom."

Leaving these two judgments to private debate, let us apply the principle to *The Grapes of Wrath*. Is this novel ethically sound? Is it a wise book? And, to revert to an earlier point, is it good sociology? One may guess from his other writings that Mr. Foerster would say "No" to all these questions. For it is undeniable that *The Grapes of Wrath* does embody a strong faith in the natural goodness of man—a doctrine abhorrent to Mr. Foerster. In Steinbeck's eyes the Joads are all good people. They may be weakly good, like Pa or Rosasharn; or they may be strongly good, like Ma Joad and Tom. But their ill fortune is never represented as due to their own tragic flaws. Conversely, all persons in power or authority—with the exception of the director of the government camp—are represented as evil. Greed creates fear, and fear creates injustice. As Steinbeck himself puts it, "The quality of owning freezes you forever into 'I' and cuts you off forever from the 'We.'"

One may admit much truth in this simple formula of good and evil and still feel that it is inadequate. The clear implication in the novel that the formula is complete, is disquieting. It arouses a suspicion that the characters—vivid as they are— are only half-truths, too. This is the more plausible, since all the real characters are drawn from one level of society. We follow the action steadily from the point of view of the Okies. People of other social strata are presented as enemies, portrayed in a single aspect, never seen from the inside.

Is this, perhaps, the clue to Edmund Wilson's comment (in *The Intent of the Critic*) that Steinbeck's novels represent almost the exact line between good and bad art? *The Grapes of Wrath* is a shrewd novel, a lively pattern of experience, varied and skillful in texture; but it may be attacked as basically sentimental. Ma Joad's remark, so effectively used to provide an ending for the Hollywood version of the story, expresses the fundamental weakness: "Rich fellas come up an' they die, and their kids ain't no good, an' they die out. But, Tom, we keep a-comin'. Don't you fret, Tom. A different time's comin'." The poor struggle for riches, success, power; but those who achieve them die out. Life is, then, a sort of squirrel cage or treadmill. Such a view gives no basis for faith in a brighter future. The assertion that the brighter future is coming—stated by Ma Joad and implied by Steinbeck—is thus mere sentimental optimism. This is a fault, by the way, ascribed to Steinbeck's more recent novel, *The Moon Is Down*.

Yet, as someone remarked, the epithet "sentimental" may easily be used as a club to beat people we don't like. I have no desire to use it as such, for the truth is that most English and

American novelists are sentimental. We are a sentimental people, and when we rebel against a conventional sentiment we get sentiment in reverse à la James T. Farrell or à la Ernest Hemingway. Or, to take more comparable material, consider for a moment Erskine Caldwell's *Tobacco Road*. Is the spectacle of total depravity offered in this production more intelligent and therefore less sentimental than the natural goodness of the downtrodden implied in *The Grapes of Wrath*? In short, while I believe that sentimentality is a valid charge against *The Grapes of Wrath*, I do not believe it is a very important one; for the sentimentality, so far as it exists, rests on an incomplete view of life, not upon frustration.

The importance of a positive quality in literature is interestingly touched upon by W. H. Auden in what I regard as the most notable essay in these two Princeton volumes. Mr. Auden [in *The Intent of the Critic*] bravely essays the difficult mission of prophecy, and in doing so he puts life first and art second. Emphasizing the interdependence of ethics, science, politics, and aesthetics, he asserts that "the attempt to make aesthetics an autonomous province has resulted in academic aesthetics, and the substitution of the pedant for the priest." In place of such exclusive specialization, the democratic society requires increasing skill in communication; for the essence of democracy, he says, is to work toward an increasingly "open" society. By an "open" society he means one in which talent and ideas have free flow.

Though Mr. Auden in this essay is prescribing for the critic, this conception of the "open" society has considerable bearing on the proper nature of art. It may be said, for instance, that *The Grapes of Wrath* is a novel vigorously sympathetic to the "open" society. The novel skillfully communicates attitudes of a relatively inarticulate group or type. It enthusiastically bridges the gap between art, politics, and ethics, making most unhappy the pedantic student of aesthetics, intent on playing the old static game of categories. In short, *The Grapes of Wrath* was

not merely a timely book on itinerant farm laborers; it was—
and is—creative in the best sense. Sentimentality may impair but
does not cancel its value. The sociological content of the novel,
far from making it an "impure" work of art, as Mr. Centeno
might wish us to believe, has, in fact, made it a more vital work
of art.

In making these tentative applications of critical theory, I
have carefully refrained from prophesying immortality for Steinbeck's novel. It may be, indeed, that we have arrived at an epoch
in which literary immortality will be unattainable. So many
books are published; so few, even of the best, are re-read; and
there are so many reading publics almost independent of one
another that the dominance required to establish a classic is
steadily more difficult to achieve. But, if classics are to emerge
from the first forty years of this century, I can think of not
more than a dozen novels in America that are so likely or such
fit candidates for that measure of immortality.

Bernard Bowron

The Grapes of Wrath:
A "Wagons West" Romance

According to the blurb of its present Bantam edition, *The
Grapes of Wrath* topped the best-seller list for two full years.
It is still going strong, as anyone knows who has observed its
perennial appeal to college students of American literature.
And with these, as probably with its original audience, the
strength of the novel's popularity seems to be almost independent of its dated message of social revolt. Even conservative
and genteel readers, though they dislike Steinbeck's naïve radi-

From *The Colorado Quarterly*, III (Summer 1954), 84-91. Drawn
from a paper read at a meeting of the Modern Language Association,
Professor Bowron's essay is reprinted by permission of the author
and of *The Colorado Quarterly*.

calism and gag over some of his calculated crudities, are taken by his novel in spite of themselves. Why should that be?

To begin with, the novel's special appeal can have little to do with its "proletarian" features. It is not even a "strike novel," in the classic sense. Though that kind of conflict plays an important part in the final section, the book as a whole is organized around a profoundly different action. Social revolt is not really Steinbeck's major concern. He has another, more universal gospel which it is designed to serve. No orthodox proletarian novelist ever generated more fury over the plight of the dispossessed, nor more sentimentality about the rise of a collective consciousness (Steinbeck's beloved "Group-Man") out of individual defeats and humiliations. We even note the regulation prophecy of an apocalyptic "final conflict" out of which, somehow, will emerge the good society. But if this novel really embodies the Party Line, then our Congressional investigators may themselves end as converts to the cause. All of Steinbeck's social message is summed up for us in Ma Joad's profound observation that "We're the people—we go on!" (She had evidently been reading Carl Sandburg.) Now, what *are* the "people"? Why do they "go on"?

In *The Grapes of Wrath* this question is answered by a famous turtle who crosses the road in Chapter Three and then proceeds to carry the symbolism of that interchapter straight into the story of the Joads' pilgrimage from Oklahoma to the western promised land. The turtle—like the Joads—is on a pilgrimage, directed by some sure, irrational instinct, to some unknown destination. He crawls along laboriously but, in Steinbeck's words, "turns aside for nothing"—neither embankment nor highway. Preacher Casy spells it out carefully for us a little later: "Nobody can't keep a turtle. . . . They work at it and work at it, and at last one day . . . away they go—off somewhere." If the Preacher had watched more closely, however, he'd have noticed that turtles don't just go vaguely "somewhere." By no means. They go "southwestward," a compass-point which Steinbeck mentions three times in one brief paragraph, in case we somehow might fail to note that turtles, like Joads, travel on Route 66.

The turtle is also indestructible. A truck hits him, and he just flips over, turns right-side up, and goes on his instinctive way. Moreover, in *his* pilgrimage the turtle is the agent of still another pilgrimage. Some wild oat seeds get stuck between his legs and shell. He carries them across the barren highway. They fall to earth on the other side, and the turtle obligingly plants them: "As the turtle crawled on down the embankment, its shell dragged dirt over the seeds." The turtle is of course the Life Force itself: tireless, indestructible, dispersing everywhere the seeds of life. But by a series of contrived associations, Steinbeck makes clear that the turtle is also the Joads—or that they are it—or in any case that "we're the people—we go on." This is hardly an original interpretation, but it has seemed to me worth restating here, simply to underline the assertion that *The Grapes of Wrath* is basically not a "proletarian" novel, in spite of Preacher Casy's strike activities and martyrdom, and Tom Joad's conversion to a kind of mystical communism. Steinbeck has the Life Force, not Marxism, on his mind.

But we must get back to the original question: what made *The Grapes of Wrath* so popular? For that question is surely not answered by the fact that its "proletarianism" is a vehicle for Steinbeck's primitivist raptures over the durability of the species, Man. This is a comforting idea, I suppose, but hardly a source of best-seller narrative excitement.

Let me approach my answer indirectly, since that was the way it came to me. Many readers must have noted that conflict and struggle—while important as a suspense device in this novel —are not by any means its most attractive feature. Nothing in the book, with the exception of a blessed interlude in a federal migrant workers' camp in California, is half so appealing as the cross-country trip itself. Bracketed dramatically by Grampa's death at the outset and Granma's on arrival in the Golden State, this trip is described in a way that is bound to appeal to any grown man who ever wanted to lay his burdens down and just go *camping*. Consider Chapter Seventeen, especially. Here while Steinbeck sets out to define the pilgrimage of the Joads and all the Okies as a cellular embryonic development of the organic society of the species, he actually presents, instead, an idyll of the simple, thoughtless, irresponsible life of people released temporarily from their daily concerns. The loving care that Steinbeck exerts on this section of his novel, and his reluctance to leave it and carry the Joads on into the conflicts that lie ahead, remind one strongly of certain other novels familiar to all American readers. These novels are not about Okies—though often they deal with the Okies of a former day, those stalwart, ungenteel and indestructible Missouri men known as "Pikes," who cross the plains and mountains in every "Wagons West" romance. Indeed, it was Guthrie's recent best-seller, *The Way West,* which opened my eyes to the real literary form of Steinbeck's *Grapes of Wrath* and to the reason for its endless appeal. Then I glanced backward some thirty years to Emerson Hough's *Covered Wagon.* That did it. *The Grapes of Wrath* is in the same genre. It derives from the "Westward" novel both the structure and the values that give it its emotional horsepower. Why shouldn't this novel be popular? It always has been—whether written by Steinbeck or by Stewart Edward White.

Well, this isn't much of a discovery, nor do I put in any claim to the originality of a thing so self-evident. One must assume that Steinbeck himself was perfectly aware that his Joads —and his turtles—were re-enacting the great American legend. He is an author much given to seeing his contemporary materials in the symbolic light of such re-enactments, and the mid-nineteenth century trek to the Pacific takes on for him in another novel [sic] *The Long Valley,* a very mythic quality indeed. In this book, published just a year before *The Grapes of Wrath,* Steinbeck has an aging pioneer speak of the great journey in a way that brings vividly to mind the Joads, and the meaning of their passage across the continent. "It wasn't Indians that were important," says the old man, "nor adventures, nor even getting out there. . . . When we saw the mountains at last, we cried—all of us. But it wasn't getting here that mattered, it was movement and westering. We carried life out here and set it down the way those ants carry eggs. . . . The westering was big as God."

Steinbeck's debt to the "Wagons West" genre may be obvious, but the extent of his debt has never been sufficiently appreciated. Yet it is striking, once one sets about examining *The Grapes of Wrath* with that parallel in mind.

First of all, the Joads travel in a covered wagon. True, it is an improvised truck, but Steinbeck very carefully calls attention to the rigging up of a tarpaulin cover to enclose the family living-space in the rear. Moreover, this wreck of an automobile is in such bad shape that one hardly thinks of it as machinery. Certainly the Joads do not. They regard it with affection and concern, and they minister to its needs till it becomes a living thing, a member of the family. The truck is both their covered wagon and their ox team. And, as with the oxen of all these westering romances, the truck's weariness and infirmities provide one unfailing device for suspense, especially in the fearful crossing of the Mohave Desert. By the traditional miracle, it barely manages to stagger across desert and mountains to the western Eden. But its hooves are mighty sore.

The main link between *The Grapes of Wrath* and its parent genre is, of course, Steinbeck's handling of the long trek itself: its use, that is, both as unfailing source of episode and as the formal, or structural, principle that holds the novel together and moves it along. In a novel like Guthrie's *The Way West* or Hough's *Covered Wagon,* the journey involves two major thematic movements. From the jumping-off place to the valley of the Platte things go pretty well. An occasional Indian skirmish provides excitement, but the real dangers lie ahead. This is the idyllic part of the trip, the "camping-out" part, where man proudly toughens up, communes with nature, and sings happy folk songs around the campfire under the western stars. So far, so good; and the author is a bit sad to pass on to the next movement of his piece. But now the high plains and the mountains and the deserts must be crossed. The Indian attacks are serious now, punishing, and the going is terrible. This is the agony which earns the promised land. The promised land itself hardly figures in such tales, except that one does finally get there. And that ends it.

The Joads' pilgrimage follows this formula, but with a difference that is, narratively, much to Steinbeck's advantage, because it allows him to continue his story, with heightened excitement, right where the traditional "Westward-Ho" novel has to stop. Since the Joads' Garden of the West is already preempted, they must continue their harassed journey indefinitely, in search of a homestead that never materializes. *The Grapes of Wrath* could theoretically go on forever. It almost does. What Steinbeck has done with the westward-journey formula is simple but ingenious. His pre-Platte movement extends up to the border of California, and the counter-movement of agonized effort and cruel Indian forays is transplanted right into the western haven itself.

Although the Joads do not cross *their* hundredth meridian until they arrive at Needles, California, this "first half" of their journey otherwise runs true to form. We get the conventional note of pathos-confirming-high-endeavor when Grampa dies at the close of the first day out, unable to stand the shock of transplanting. He is then buried in the regulation nameless grave on the trail, and Steinbeck pointedly has the Joads conceal his fresh grave from the prying eyes of the redskins, by strewing leaves over it. (In this case, as elsewhere in *The Grapes of Wrath*, the state troopers function as latter-day redskins—cruel, inhuman beings, never to be trusted for a minute. Tom Joad knows that if they find Grampa's illegally buried corpse, they will make trouble.)

But sadness is only a minor theme of this "first half" of the traditional journey, which typically stresses the life-affirming impact of the westering experience upon the people involved in it. Steinbeck goes right along with the formula. The Joads meet and join up with the Wilsons, and thus we get a wagon train—or, to go a step farther (and this also is strictly in the genre), we get an embryonic society: uprooted men shed the old society, and during the rejuvenating continent-crossing they create a new one, a "good" one, ministering to simple but immemorial human needs. Out of this social compact formed in a state of nature, new "leaders" emerge. In the Joads' case, Ma takes over, surprising herself as much as her men-folk by her new stature—which she achieves (as all "Wagons West" leaders must) by forcibly taking charge in a situation threatening the cohesion and safety of the new wagon-train society. Ma Joad, brandishing her jackhandle at Pa, is an archetypical character.

And the society she rules behaves as predictably as she does. It adjusts its ways to the primitive life of the trail (not much of a trick for the Joads—but at least they had left behind the simple amenities of a permanent shelter and a cookstove). This wagon-train meets others, and celebrates these occasions with folk songs and rude goodfellowship. It temporarily breaks down, too, of course—a burned-out bearing substituting for a broken wagon wheel or moribund ox team. It overcomes such difficulty by the usual communal effort, demonstrating the viability of its social compact. Nothing can stop this westward movement.

Unfortunately, no courtship occurs during this first phase of the journey. Maybe Steinbeck felt he was being orthodox enough without going all the way. However, the incessant love-making of Rose of Sharon and her new husband, Connie, provides a somewhat similar, though less genteel, titillation. Unfortunately, too (though as we've seen, necessarily), Grampa had to die at the outset. Otherwise we would have had in him a workable facsimile of the regulation mountain-man—not, of course, in the role of a trusted guide but in that of a hearty vulgarian, a combination of the sentimental literary "grotesque" and the prankish Sut Lovingood protagonist of western humor. But these are minor and allowable omissions. The Joads' westering exhibits all the really necessary ingredients of the first act of the genre.

The Joads' "second act," as I said earlier, represents a geographic displacement of the "tragic" phase of the genre, since Steinbeck, for his own very good reasons, stages it *within* the longed-for Western Garden. The customary shift to suffering and desperation is abruptly announced at the California state line. This involves not only the crossing of the Mohave Desert, during which Granma so spectacularly gives out, but several important preliminary incidents as well, which occur during the Joads' breathing spell (also customary) on the Colorado River before they tackle the climactic dangers ahead. Here the prized solidarity of this modern wagon-train is at last disrupted. Noah Joad—the loony son—deserts the party to wander aimlessly down-river, because, as he explains, "I can't leave this here water." (Why did Steinbeck have Noah do this particular crazy thing? One hopes the author had more in mind than a biblical association of "Noah" and "water." Maybe he was making one more concession to his story-formula, wherein the most faint-hearted pioneers turn back from the arid strangeness of the lands beyond the hundredth meridian.) Here, too, the other family that completed the Joad wagon train is halted by the imminent death of a frail and suffering wife. And here—if I may be allowed to press my analogy all the way—the first "Indian attack" occurs, when a blustering and pitiless California state trooper threatens the Joads, so that they must give up their needed two-day rest and plunge ahead into the desert to escape his renewed onslaught, scheduled for the next morning.

For a moment, when the Joad caravan laboriously tops its last mountain pass and gazes out over the incredibly beautiful, fruitful valley of its dreams, the West has been won. "God Almighty," Pa intones in his role of the fulfilled pioneer, ". . . I never knowed there was anything like her. . . . Ma, come look.

We're there!" Steinbeck's prose at this point achieves Hollywood lushness as he labors to produce a heightened composite image of Everyman's vision of the Garden of the West. It looks like Paradise. Only it isn't. And Pa Joad is sadly wrong. They are not "there" at last, and they never will be. Their real time of troubles—corresponding to the desperate second act of the "Covered Wagon" romances—has hardly begun.

There is no need, here, to examine this concluding section of *The Grapes of Wrath,* in which Steinbeck departs from the strict form of his genre while retaining much of its spirit. The point is that the great trek is concluded and yet in another sense has just begun. Out of this irony and frustration Steinbeck distills his "wrath." Not—be it well understood—so much the Joads' wrath as our own. For the fact is that a reader is more frustrated than the Joads. It is a literary frustration, to be sure, but one with the strongest and most dependable emotional overtones. And it testifies to the great artfulness—I do not say great art—of *The Grapes of Wrath.*

Steinbeck's book is a triumph of literary engineering. What makes *The Grapes of Wrath* a popular novel also gives it its emotional high voltage. The "Covered Wagon" romance-formula requires the *winning* of the West. A homestead at the end of the trail is the only appropriate reward for so much agony. By providing the formula, without the reward, Steinbeck makes the plight of his modern pioneers utterly outrageous, precisely because it does outrage the genre ending. For Steinbeck's purpose, western fiction was far more useful than any mere western fact. It enabled him to outdo spectacularly the standardized police brutality and capitalist villainy in the ordinary "proletarian" strike novel of the 1930s. He did it with half the effort and twice the wrath.

Warren French
Another Look at The Grapes of Wrath

As John Steinbeck reminds us in the introduction to *Cannery Row,* what we call people depends upon the keyhole through which we see them. Since books are projections of people, what we call them, too, depends upon the way we look at them. They do not look alike to everybody; a book is likely to endure, in fact, because it provokes argument. Since books can be seen through many peepholes, any reader is entitled to air his own opinions about them, but confusing one's private opinion with a universal reaction may leave one in an untenable position.

What makes a "best-seller" is one of the most deceptively complex problems in the psychology of literary taste. When analyzing the reception of a successful book of even the recent past, ignoring changes in the intellectual milieu may lead to conclusions that are superficially appealing, yet basically unacceptable, as are those Bernard Bowron advances about *The Grapes of Wrath.* I would like to take exception to his theories, which I feel are forced upon rather than developed from the book and which I maintain misrepresent its relationship to other tales of the American West.

Bowron's article may be summarized by the statements that *The Grapes of Wrath* belongs to a genre of "wagons westward" romances and that it has enjoyed a huge sale because of its exploitations of the conventions of this genre. The author draws adroit parallels between incidents in the book and what he asserts are the principal conventions of the genre, but he advances no evidence that these alleged similarities contributed to the reception of the book. Indeed his conclusions only raise the further problem of determining why the book should have been

From *The Colorado Quarterly,* III (Winter 1955), 337-343. Reprinted by permission of *The Colorado Quarterly.*

more popular than others of the same kind. Actually I believe that Bowron has overlooked the real relationship between *The Grapes of Wrath* and "covered-wagon" fiction, since Steinbeck, far from capitalizing upon the conventions of this genre, refutes them.

It takes more than a covered wagon to make a genre. Bowron implies that all writers about covered wagons follow the same well-worn trail, whereas many covered-wagon novels resemble each other because the vehicle is but one of many means to a common end. Novels like *The Way West* are only a few of many eulogizing the conquest of the unknown. Zane Grey, veteran contributor to the genre, made the pony express, the trans-continental railroad, and a telegraph line perform the same functions as the wagon train. The same pattern Grey followed can be found today with fantastic trimmings in much of the science-fiction about the subjugation of remote planets. Nor did the genre originate with the flood of tales about our West. It is at least as old as the Biblical tale of the Exodus and as the *Odyssey;* a spiritualized version provides the framework for *The Pilgrim's Progress.* Since Steinbeck is known to follow classical models (Arthurian legends in *Tortilla Flat,* the Genesis story in *East of Eden*), he might have been more likely to turn to Moses than to Emerson Hough if he needed a model for a tale about man's attempt to win the promised land. But actually *The Grapes of Wrath* satirizes rather than conforms to this genre, because it outrages all the psychological assumptions upon which such stories rely for their appeal.*

Bowron acknowledges that Steinbeck frustrates the readers' expectations of a conventional reward, but he ignores the psychological underpinnings of these romances that demand this denouement. In the first place, such stories concern a dissatisfied and frustrated hero who is innately superior to a society

* Using Bowron's method, one would have to argue that *Gulliver's Travels* is popular because Swift conforms to the genre of the travel book.—Ed.

which fails to recognize his merits. Thus dissatisfied and frustrated readers, touchy about their own unrewarded virtues, can identify the hero's problems with their own and share vicariously in his struggle to attain the distant paradise where merit will receive its due. To establish himself, the hero undergoes a series of trials; once these are over, however, and the promised land is reached, it is the unspoiled place that fulfills his fondest expectations and is either vacant or occupied by a weaker and easily conquered group. In addition to being based upon this unvarying pattern of frustration, ordeal, and triumph, such novels are set in a remote period. They echo the legend of a Golden Age and are fundamentally primitivistic and anti-intellectual. Primitivistic, because they concern a simpler world than the readers'; anti-intellectual, because their hero is not called upon to develop in order to meet the challenge of new situations, but rather encounters situations that can be altered to suit his tailor-made capacities. His character is static; the only movement in the book is physical. Writer and reader tacitly agree beforehand that the hero unquestionably deserves a reward and are concerned only with his struggles to attain it.

The Grapes of Wrath fails to satisfy this formula. Steinbeck's migrants are not escapists, but refugees. (James Thurber included in *Fables for Our Times* a tale about rabbits that concisely illustrates the difference between these groups.) Escapist readers could derive little satisfaction from identifying themselves with the Joads. Furthermore, as Bowron concedes, their troubles begin only after they have arrived at what they suppose will be their promised land. I cannot agree that Steinbeck is reluctant to conclude the description of the migration; most of the action occurs in California, and only enough is said of the trip westward to illustrate the process of the migrants welding themselves into a group. *The Grapes of Wrath* really begins at the point where *The Covered Wagon* ends, for in the Exodus genre, it is assumed that everyone will live happily ever after, at least for a while.

Steinbeck, furthermore, does not describe a remote situation but a contemporary one. For the details he used, he needed no literary model except his own factual account of the migration, *Their Blood Is Strong.* He was concerned not with idealizing the past but with symbolizing the present. Nor is the book based upon any concept of the innate superiority of the migrants. They were largely responsible for their own troubles, both at home and on the road. Since they had to learn through humiliating experiences, the complacent mediocrity can derive no consolation from the bitter record of their adventures. The anti-intellectuals, with their reliance upon formulas, are represented by some of the Californians, with whom there is reason to believe offended readers did identify themselves.

Finally, the book is not primitivistic. Critics have shed much ink over Steinbeck's primitivism, but they have conveniently ignored a key passage in *The Grapes of Wrath:*

> This you may say of man—when theories change and crash, when schools, philosophies, when narrow dark alleys of thought, national, religious, economic, groan and disintegrate —man reaches, stumbles forward, painfully, mistakenly sometimes. Having stepped forward, he may slip back, but only half a step, never the full step back.

Steinbeck's distaste for primitivism is further illustrated by his treatment of Noah Joad, the brother who disappears at the border of the promised land. Bowron puzzles over the significance of Noah, but the meaning of his disappearance seems clear if one concedes that Steinbeck is not exalting the merits of the primitive. Noah is a true primitive; his wishes are fulfilled by a simple reunion with beneficent nature. Steinbeck, however, is not interested in such a solution to the problems posed by the migration. Noah's disappearance from the book implies that the man who does not stumble forward, vanishes.

Thus the whole psychological basis of the book is designed to frustrate the anticipations of the reader geared to the smoothly executed clichés of western genre fiction. Structural similarities between *The Grapes of Wrath* and *The Covered Wagon* can be found, but it is hard to believe that Steinbeck accepted the same set of values as Emerson Hough. If Steinbeck gave any thought to the "wagons westward" genre, it was to reflect that such books were myths designed to confirm a pattern of response inapplicable to the realities of his own time.*

Bowron suggests that while Steinbeck must have been aware that his migrants were re-enacting the Great American Legend he deliberately suppressed the parallel in order to put something over on his readers. One does not need, however, "to assume" that Steinbeck was aware of the parallel; he went to some pains to emphasize it and the influence of the earlier tradition upon his characters. The Joads describe themselves as immediate descendants of the pioneers who made the original conquest. "Grampa took up the land," Pa Joad observes, "and he had to kill the Indians and drive them away." Rationalizing the need for leaving his homestead, Pa further recalls the motives of his ancestors and observes that people are moving because "They want somepin better'n what they got. An' that's the on'y way they'll ever git it. Wantin' it an' needin' it, they'll go out an' git it." The parallel between California and the Edens of the past is also clearly emphasized by Pa's hopeful meditation, " 'Course it'll be all different out there—plenty work, an' ever'thing nice an' green, an' little white houses an' oranges growin' around." The parallel, however, exists only in the minds of the characters; Steinbeck, when he speaks for himself, emphasizes the futility of their expectations:

> They had hoped to find a home, and they found only hatred;
> . . . perhaps the owners had heard from their grandfathers
> how easy it is to steal land from a soft man if you are fierce
> and hungry and armed. The owners hated them.

* In *Of Mice and Men*, Steinbeck speaks knowingly of "those Western magazines ranch men love to read and scoff at and secretly believe."—Ed.

I have already suggested that Steinbeck did not need to draw this parallel from the conventions of Western fiction, since he had ample historic parallels at hand. Western fiction may be more useful than Western fact; but since Steinbeck was acquainted with the facts, it is difficult to see why he would have to subject himself to a prolonged exposure to the writings of Stewart Edward White.

Nor were the parallels between the novel and the story of the conquest of the West so obscure that they were not perceived by early readers of the novel. Even if American critics were so preoccupied with other elements in the book that they ignored Steinbeck's ironic use of the myth of the frontier, the reviewer for the London *Times* observed in September 1939:

> While lesser American writers complacently recall their country's past, Mr. Steinbeck is anxiously in touch with its present. He, too, describes an exodus to the West, but this is made in ramshackle motor-cars instead of lumbering wagons. Here there are no battles to bring glory, and at the end the land of promise is a bitter disappointment. There, sure enough, are the farms and orchards and well-watered lands, but others are in possession of them.

Here are Bowron's comparisons with the "wagons westward" genre, but with the emphasis placed upon Steinbeck's refutation rather than his confirmation of the anticipations aroused by such works. *The Grapes of Wrath* may be accurately read as an attempt (unsuccessful, of course, in view of the inertia of confirmed romancers) to explode rather than perpetuate the myths and conventions upon which Western genre fiction are based.

To attribute the novel's popularity, however, even to its turning upside-down the "covered wagon" dream, Bowron would have to prove either that the readers who lap up traditional romance would be enthusiastic about a book that outraged their preconceptions or that the persons who have read and remained interested in Steinbeck's novel were primarily attracted by the passages describing the migration. Since neither contention appears tenable, I see no reason why either should be accepted unless no plausible alternative can be advanced.

While reviewers do not always mirror public taste, an examination of the American reviews of the book suggest a reason for its popularity. It is difficult even now to reconstruct the intellectual milieu of the 1930s, because the war and the period of postwar uncertainties have made us strangers to our own past. In the present era of increasing indifferent conformity in national affairs and increasing preoccupation with international tensions, one forgets that only fifteen years ago isolationism was as common as widespread absorption in national scandals. The American public is not as violent as it used to be. Compare, for example, contemporary reactions to the Lindbergh and Greenlease kidnapings. Even Senator McCarthy has not provoked as much uproar as the late Senator Bilbo.

When *The Grapes of Wrath* appeared, it was most frequently compared to *Uncle Tom's Cabin,* another novel that became a storm center by virtue of its outspoken airing of social and of sectional antipathies. Both provided an outlet not for escapists but for agitators and counter-agitators. Steinbeck's book even provoked, like Mrs. Stowe's, a series of now almost unknown "answers." Bowron's observation that the book's popularity with genteel readers could not be attributed to its naïve radicalism appears to be based upon the assumption that everyone who was excited about the book agreed with it. Contemporary comments, especially from Oklahoma and California, suggest that it attracted much of its audience in the same way as books banned in Boston.

Throughout Bowron's article, he attempts to explain away the success of *The Grapes of Wrath* by ignoring most of the themes that entered into its composition in order to concentrate upon an overemphasis of one debatable parallel. His two key observations, "nothing in the book is half so appealing as the cross-country trip" and "there is no point in examining the second part," are entirely subjective. Most interpreters have ignored the cross-country trip in their rush to get into an argument over the second part of the book. The argument might be advanced that readers have not been so much hoodwinked by a deft but superficial craftsman as that they have ignored the universal elements in the narrative in order to concentrate upon the transient and the particular. Bowron's artfully formulated analogies provide skillful justification for a personal distaste for the book, but I doubt that they contribute much to an analysis of the psychology of public taste.

Theodore Pollock
On the Ending of The Grapes of Wrath

Although *The Grapes of Wrath* has been accepted by students and critics as a respectable—even praiseworthy—addition to the literature of social protest, it has only reluctantly and somewhat embarrassedly been treated as a work of art. The ending in particular has proved a source of disaffection among careful readers, who find it either offensively sentimental or not really an ending at all. It seems to me that Steinbeck wrought more with his ending than may at first be apparent, and I should like to consider, therefore, a theme that threads its way throughout *The Grapes of Wrath*—an important theme that is successfully and artfully concluded at the book's close—the theme of reproduction.

Generally, of course, the book follows the most basic of structural patterns, that of the picaresque tradition. This time, however, instead of an individual (or two) taking to the road in search of adventure, we have an entire family, representing three generations, with the promise of a fourth in the form of

From *Modern Fiction Studies*, IV (Summer 1958), 177-178. Reprinted by permission of the Purdue Research Foundation.

the pregnant Rose of Sharon, traveling out of a search for a means of survival. As the book opens, a description of drought immediately sets the tone of sterility; Chapter One is peppered with references to the sun, ants, weeds, dust, and wind, and the colors red and gray predominate. Dead corn lies scattered about. Rain in sufficient quantity has not fallen on mother earth. On the cosmic level, then, there is no reproduction.

When we meet the Joad family, we are early apprised of the importance of Ma Joad. She is the true leader of the family, keeping it together under the most trying of experiences; but following the folkways of her people, she subordinates herself to Pa Joad and, at the beginning at least, has little to say at the family council. Rose of Sharon, the only other important female character in the novel, only gradually takes on importance. Firstly, she serves throughout the book as a human clock, a timekeeper, and all the action of *The Grapes of Wrath* takes place within the temporal confines of her pregnancy. Secondly and more importantly, she early offers herself as a convenient symbol in contrast to mother earth. Whereas earth has grown unproductive, the people have not, and Rose of Sharon's pregnancy, a living symbol of hope and immortality, becomes progressively more important to a complete understanding of what Steinbeck is doing.

As the Joad family drives across the country, it is subjected to a series of jolts, natural, mechanical, and social. Grampa and Granma die; Noah walks into oblivion; the automobile breaks down from time to time; the family treasury continually diminishes; not all the people met along the way take kindly to the intruders from Oklahoma. As these pressures mount, the figure of Ma Joad increasingly assumes importance until, in her precedent-shattering rebellion, she wrests control of the family from Pa. The apotheosis of the *Ewig-Weibliche,* she hustles about, bolstering the flagging spirits of the men, tending to Tom's weakening sense of social integrity, catering to the natural doubts and distresses of Rose of Sharon, all the while somehow managing to provide food for the family. She knows that the secret of life is the province of woman, and Rose of Sharon, actually undergoing the tribulations of that secret, keeps it ever before us.

Then why is the infant stillborn? Has Steinbeck insisted that "the people go on" only to rob the reader of the vision of life being handed from one generation to another? In short, is *The Grapes of Wrath* basically a pessimistic book? It is here, I think, that we must examine the last chapter in the light of the first, keeping in mind the juxtaposition of mother earth to Rose of Sharon. Dramatic necessity compelled Steinbeck to kill the infant, of course, but there is another reason. The breast-feeding of a fifty-year-old stranger by Rose of Sharon has been generally condemned as rank sentimentalism, and perhaps there is something overdone about this obvious "milk of human kindness" symbolism.

But consider the elemental background of this scene. It occurs during a gigantic storm, the rain of which has almost inundated the boxcar the Joads now share with another family. It is as if the human sacrifice of Rose of Sharon's baby has removed the curse of sterility from the cosmos. The baby dies as the result of *past* occurrences. But if Chapter One was all drought and despair, Chapter Thirty is all water and hope, on a super-Joad level.*

It is plain, then—to me at least—that *The Grapes of Wrath* is an optimistic book—and it is equally plain that it is a well-constructed one.

* It might also be argued, however, in view of the similarity between the drought and downpour imagery in *The Grapes of Wrath* and T. S. Eliot's *The Waste Land* that Steinbeck's final point is that too much water can be as destructive as too little—that men cannot depend at all upon capricious nature to alleviate human misery, but must develop a compassionate responsibility for each other. Far from invalidating Mr. Pollock's conclusion, this argument strengthens it by providing justification for Rose of Sharon's act of mercy.—Ed.

Bibliography
and Index

Bibliography

1. WHAT WAS THE DUST BOWL?

A QUARTER OF A CENTURY AFTER THE DARK DAYS OF THE 1930s, no definitive history of the dust bowl had yet appeared. Vance Johnson's *Heaven's Tableland: The Dust Bowl Story* (New York: Farrar, Straus, 1947) is, in the words of the author—an Amarillo, Texas, newspaperman, who reported the great storms—"a tale about man's struggle to control a unique, enticing, merciless section of our country known as the Southern Great Plains." For junior-high-school students, a prolific author of children's books, Patricia Lauber, has prepared *Dust Bowl: the Story of Man on the Great Plains* (New York: Coward-McCann, 1958), which is illustrated with photographs and maps by Wes McKeown.

Magazines of the mid-thirties carried many illustrated accounts of devastation in the dust bowl. Its history may be traced through short notices in *Time, Newsweek,* and *Business Week.* Especially useful in "Grasslands: The Frontier, Cultivation, Dust," prepared by the Editors of *Fortune* (November 1935, pp. 58-67). Another letter from Mrs. Caroline Henderson appears in the *Atlantic Monthly*, June 1937, pp. 715-17.

A memorable pictorial record is preserved in *Land of the Free* (New York: Harcourt, Brace, 1938), which also contains a poetic narrative by Archibald MacLeish, based on the pictures, and in Pare Lorentz's documentary motion picture *The Plow That Broke the Plains*. The making of this controversial government-sponsored film is discussed in "Documented Dust," *Time*, May 25, 1936, p. 47-48.

2. WHO WERE THE "OKIES"?

One of the earliest accounts of the migration is "Again the Covered Wagon" by Paul S. Taylor, the University of California economist who is one of the outstanding authorities on California's agrarian problems (*Survey Graphic*, July 1935, pp. 348-51). Also outstanding among contemporary accounts is "New Oregon Trail: Drought Refugees in Search of New Farms" by Richard Neuberger, later a United States Senator from Oregon (*Collier's*, March 27, 1937, pp. 14-15).

Still regarded as the most authoritative accounts of California's troubles with the "Okies," as well as the migratory labor problem in the United States in general, are Carey McWilliams' *Factories in the Field* and his *Ill Fares the Land* (Boston: Little, Brown, 1942). Both contain extensive bibliographies.

Those interested in digging out the story of the migrants and their reception from the voluminous reports of the proceedings of the La Follette Committee, cited by McWilliams, should consult *The United States Senate Education and Labor Committee Hearings on Violations of Free Speech and Assembly and Infractions of the Rights of Labor*, Parts 46-75 (Washington: Government Printing Office, 1939-1940).

A survey of the situation of the migrant worker in California more recent than McWilliams' books is Lloyd

Horace Fisher's *Harvest Labor Market in California* (Cambridge, Mass.: Harvard University Press, 1953).

Only pictures can make fully clear, however, the plight of the migrants in the thirties. Besides those taken by Horace Bristol for *Life* (June 5, 1939, pp. 66-67; February 19, 1940, pp. 10-11), an excellent group by Dorothea Lange (Mrs. Paul S. Taylor) is contained in her *An American Exodus: A Record of Human Erosion* (New York: Reynal and Hitchcock, 1940), which also contains a brief essay by her husband. More pictures from the files of the Farm Security Administration, which were included in an exhibition at the Museum of Modern Art in New York, are reproduced in the Museum's publication, *The Bitter Years: 1935-1941*, edited by Edward Steichen (1962).

3. What Did John Steinbeck Know About the "Okies"?

Besides *Their Blood Is Strong* and *The Grapes of Wrath*, John Steinbeck contributed an article about the "Okies," "Dubious Battle in California," to the *Nation*, September 12, 1936, pp. 302-304. Excerpts from the letters he wrote while living among the migrants appear in "Steinbeck's Way of Writing," Lewis Gannett's Introduction to *The Portable Steinbeck*, edited by Pascal Covici (New York: Viking Press, 1946). This anthology also contains "Breakfast," described as "one of many working notes made in preparation for *The Grapes of Wrath*, which was not used in the novel."

4. What Became of the Joads?

No authoritative account dealing exclusively with the absorption of the "Okies" into California's population had been published up to 1963. The story may be pieced together from the reports of the United States House of Representatives Select Committee to Investigate the Interstate Migration of Destitute Citizens' hearings in 1940, which are indexed in the *Cumulative Index of Congressional Committee Hearings of the 74th to the 85th Congress* (Washington: Government Printing Office, 1959). This group, often called the Tolan Committee, after its chairman, the Honorable John H. Tolan of Los Angeles, continued its work—and reports—as the House Select Committee Investigating National Defense Migration in 1941 and 1942.

The details of the growing shortage of agricultural labor in California during World War II may be found in the *Final Report of the Joint Legislative Fact-Finding Committee on Agricultural and Industrial Labor* of the state of California, published by the state on May 4, 1945.

5. How Was *The Grapes of Wrath* Received at Home?

A number of brief excerpts from the reviews of the novel may be found in the *Book Review Digest* for 1939. The details of the astonishing reception of the book may be gathered from weekly reports in *Publishers' Weekly* during 1939 and 1940. Some reviews in less prominent newspapers and periodicals are quoted in "Red Meat and Red Herrings," *The Commonweal*, October 13, 1939, pp. 562-63.

6. Was *The Grapes of Wrath* Answered?

The pamphlets answering Steinbeck are for the most part out of print. Peter Lisca in *The Wide World of John Steinbeck* (New Brunswick, N.J.: Rutgers University Press, 1958, pp. 148-51) quotes from them and lists other answers in his notes. The report of the joint California legislative committee cited above under "What Became of the Joads?" contains (p. 24) an angry rebuke of Steinbeck and Carey

McWilliams by R. N. Wilson, director of the California State Chamber of Commerce.

7. How Has *The Grapes of Wrath* Been Received Abroad?

The reception of the book in France and Russia has been carefully studied by American scholars. Thelma L. Smith and Ward Miner in *Transatlantic Migration* (Durham, N.C.: Duke University Press, 1955, pp. 239-45), provide a check list of French translations of Steinbeck and of articles in French on his work. Similar compilations—especially for Germany and the Scandinavian countries, where Steinbeck is much admired—would be useful. Jean-Paul Sartre discussed the French response to the novel in one of the first articles from France to appear in this country after World War II, "American Novelists in French Eyes," *Atlantic Monthly*, August 1946, pp. 114-18. Albert Gérard's *John Steinbeck* (Brussels: Ed. La Sixaine, 1947—in French) is one of the earliest monographs about the author.

Russian enthusiasm for the novel, which was the first of Steinbeck's actually to be translated into that language, is described by Deming Brown in *Soviet Attitudes toward American Writing* (Princeton, N.J.: Princeton University Press, 1962), pp. 74-80. Brown translates passages from several reviews that appeared in Russian periodicals in 1940.

Reviews of the novel in its foreign-language editions are not indexed in any source available to American readers. The annual volumes of UNESCO's *Index Translationum* (Paris) list translations published in member countries.

8. Is the Movie Like the Book?

Major reviews of the motion picture are listed in *The Reader's Guide to Periodical Literature* for 1940. Other useful discussions are listed in the bibliography of George Bluestone's *Novels into Film*.

The script of the motion picture has been reprinted in *Twenty Best Film Plays*, edited by John Gassner and Dudley Nichols (New York: Crown Publishers, 1943).

An interesting treatment of the story of the Joads in still another medium is Woody Guthrie's ballad, "Tom Joad," which is reprinted in his *American Folksong* (New York: Oak Publishers, 1963), pp. 24-25. Guthrie notes that he wrote his seventeen-stanza song in New York the night that he saw the motion picture. He compresses a surprising number of details from the story into irregularly rhymed five-line stanzas.

9. Is *The Grapes of Wrath* ART OR PROPAGANDA?

Complementary analyses of the novel are contained in: Peter Lisca's *The Wide World of John Steinbeck* (New Brunswick, N.J.: Rutgers University Press, 1958), which concentrates on the relationship of the inter-chapters to the main narrative; and Warren French's *John Steinbeck* (New York: Twayne Publishers, 1961) which treats the main narrative about the Joads as the account not of a frustrating physical migration, but a triumphant "education of the heart." A new book, *John Steinbeck*, by Joseph Fontenrose, a distinguished student of classical myths at the University of California (Berkeley), is included in the American Authors and Critics Series (Barnes and Noble).

Several of the most valuable essays about the novel are collected in *Steinbeck and His Critics*, edited by E. W. Tedlock, Jr., and C. V. Wicker (Albuquerque: University of New Mexico Press, 1957), including Frederic I. Carpenter's "The Philosophical Joads" and a chapter from Joseph

Warren Beach's *American Fiction, 1920-1940.* The anthology also includes Martin Staples Shockley's "Christian Symbolism in *The Grapes of Wrath,*" reprinted from *College English*, November 1956, pp. 87-90, and several statements by John Steinbeck himself, among them "A Letter on Criticism" reprinted from the *Colorado Quarterly*, Autumn 1955.

An extensive list of critical articles about *The Grapes of Wrath* appears in *The American Novel 1789-1959*, edited by Donna Gerstenberger and George Hendrick (Denver: Alan Swallow, 1961). Especially worthy of note is the discussion of the anachronism of Steinbeck's agrarian thinking in an increasingly industrialized society, in Chester E. Eisinger's "Jeffersonian Agrarianism in *The Grapes of Wrath*," *University of Kansas City Review*, Winter 1957, pp. 149-54.

Since the compilation of the Gerstenberger-Hendrick bibliography, Walter Fuller Taylor has summed up the case against the religious and economic philosophies behind the novel in "*The Grapes of Wrath* Reconsidered," *Mississippi Quarterly*, Summer 1959, pp. 136-44. J. Paul Hunter's essay, "Steinbeck's Wine of Affirmation in *The Grapes of Wrath*" appears in *Stetson Studies in the Humanities Number One* (Deland, Fla.: Stetson University Press, 1963). "Some Pervasive Motifs in *The Grapes of Wrath*" by Robert J. Griffin and William Freedman was published in the *Journal of English and German Philology* in July 1963, and a special issue of *Modern Fiction Studies*, devoted entirely to Steinbeck and containing an extensive bibliography of writings about him, was projected for autumn 1964.

Index

FOR THE BEST IN PAPERBACKS, LOOK FOR THE 🐧

In every corner of the world, on every subject under the sun, Penguin represents quality and variety—the very best in publishing today.

For complete information about books available from Penguin—including Pelicans, Puffins, Peregrines, and Penguin Classics—and how to order them, write to us at the appropriate address below. Please note that for copyright reasons the selection of books varies from country to country.

In the United Kingdom: For a complete list of books available from Penguin in the U.K., please write to *Dept E.P., Penguin Books Ltd, Harmondsworth, Middlesex, UB7 0DA*.

In the United States: For a complete list of books available from Penguin in the U.S., please write to *Dept BA, Penguin*, Box 999, Bergenfield, New Jersey 07621-0999.

In Canada: For a complete list of books available from Penguin in Canada, please write to *Penguin Books Canada Ltd, 2801 John Street, Markham, Ontario L3R 1B4*.

In Australia: For a complete list of books available from Penguin in Australia, please write to the *Marketing Department, Penguin Books Australia Ltd, P.O. Box 257, Ringwood, Victoria 3134*.

In New Zealand: For a complete list of books available from Penguin in New Zealand, please write to the *Marketing Department, Penguin Books (NZ) Ltd, Private Bag, Takapuna, Auckland 9*.

In India: For a complete list of books available from Penguin, please write to *Penguin Overseas Ltd, 706 Eros Apartments, 56 Nehru Place, New Delhi, 110019*.

In Holland: For a complete list of books available from Penguin in Holland, please write to *Penguin Books Nederland B.V., Postbus 195, NL–1380AD Weesp, Netherlands*.

In Germany: For a complete list of books available from Penguin, please write to *Penguin Books Ltd, Friedrichstrasse 10–12, D–6000 Frankfurt Main 1, Federal Republic of Germany*.

In Spain: For a complete list of books available from Penguin in Spain, please write to *Longman Penguin España, Calle San Nicolas 15, E–28013 Madrid, Spain*.

In Japan: For a complete list of books available from Penguin in Japan, please write to *Longman Penguin Japan Co Ltd, Yamaguchi Building, 2-12-9 Kanda Jimbocho, Chiyoda-Ku, Tokyo 101, Japan*.